The Life of
BLESSED MARGARET
of
CASTELLO

1287 - 1320

by
Father William R. Bonniwell, O.P.

Illustrations by
Father Patrick Marrin, O.P.

"For my father and my mother have left me: but the Lord hath taken me up."

—Psalm 26:10

TAN Books
Charlotte, North Carolina

Nihil Obstat:	Thomas T. Shea, O.P.
	Bruce A. Williams, O.P.
Imprimi Potest:	Terence Quinn, O.P., Prior Provincial
	St. Joseph Province
	New York, New York
Nihil Obstat:	Thomas G. Doran
	Censor Deputatus
Imprimatur	✠ Arthur J. O'Neil
	Bishop of Rockford
	February 22, 1979

The *Nihil Obstat* and *Imprimatur* are official declarations that a book or pamphlet is free of doctrinal or moral error. No implication is contained therein that those who have granted the *Nihil Obstat* and *Imprimatur* agree with the contents, opinions or statements expressed.

Originally published in 1952 as *The Story of Margaret of Metola* by P. J. Kenedy & Sons, New York, New York. Published (revised) as *The Life of Margaret of Castello* in 1955 in Ireland by Clonmore & Reynolds Ltd., Dublin, and in England by Burns Oates and Washbourne Ltd., London. Second edition (revised) published as *The Life of Blessed Margaret of Castello* by IDEA, Inc. in 1979. Third edition (revised again) co-published in 1983 by TAN Books, and IDEA, Inc., P.O. Box 4010, Madison, Wisconsin 53711 (also P.O. Box 119, Elmwood Park, Illinois 60635).

Copyright © 1952 by P. J. Kenedy & Sons, New York.

Copyright © 1979 by IDEA, Inc.

Library of Congress Catalog Card No.: 83-70524

ISBN: 978-0-89555-213-6

Cover drawing by Richard Lewis, Rockford, Illinois, based on the statue of Blessed Margaret in the Blessed Margaret Shrine at the Church of St. Louis Bertrand, Louisville, Kentucky. Statue by Tony Moroder, Moroder International, Milwaukee, Wisconsin.

All rights reserved. No part of this book may be reproduced or transmitted in any form or by any means, electronic or mechanical, including photocopying, recording, or by any information storage or retrieval system, without permission in writing from IDEA, Inc.

Printed and bound in the United States of America.

TAN Books
Charlotte, North Carolina
www.TANBooks.com
2014

TABLE OF CONTENTS

Blessed Margaret of Castello, beatified on October 19, 1609. Her feast day is April 13th. The statue is in Blessed Margaret's shrine at the Church of St. Louis Bertrand in Louisville, Kentucky.

PREFACE

This third edition in thirty-one years of Father William R. Bonniwell's *Life of Blessed Margaret of Castello,* the second since 1979, is something of a phenomenon.

It is not unusual that the passage of more than a quarter-century sees many changes in the life of the Church in the modern world. But in some sectors of the Church's life, the events following (but not necessarily resulting from) the Second Vatican Council swept in on winds of violence that not only brought some "fresh air" into its rooms, but threatened at times almost to push the Church away from its foundation and crush it! Not everything "blowin' in the wind" in post-Vatican II days is the *Holy* Spirit, we know, and not every "prophet" in fact *is* one.

One aspect of the life of the Church that apparently has suffered to some degree is its traditional devotion to the saints. This age has taken countless secular heroes and heroines to its heart, and for the most part, has been disappointed. It has taken up cause after cause in sincere attempts to better the world and the lives of those who inhabit it, but all too often this was done misguidedly, within the parameters of some merely secular "salvation" divorced from the Cross and the power of Him who hangs upon and has overcome it.

No wonder then, that far from being bettered by attempts to save itself by itself, society seems on the contrary to have disintegrated a bit more "in the widening gyre," and appears as well to have become a victim of its own increasingly morbid fascination with self. And from that quarter salvation can never come.

The great masters of the life of the Spirit have known and written for ages that one of the first consequences of the loss of personal focus on God and the things of God is the *failure to pray*—whether the prayer of praise, of thanksgiving, of petition or of intercession. As one's faith weakens and diminishes, one's vision of God in prayer becomes blurred, and the simple, daily converse with Him falls by the way. Inevitably, then, other interests push in to fill the void, and the darker side of human nature comes to the fore in a rush of materialism. "The best lack all conviction, while the worst are filled with passionate intensity; the blood-dimmed tide is loosed, and everywhere the ceremony of innocence is drowned."

So it is now. Every decade in this century has seen the increasing (and increasingly blatant) disregard for all human rights, and especially for the most basic right, the right to life itself.

Aided and abetted by courts and legislatures, and *followed* by some political and religious "leaders," the social planners and multimillion dollar foundation grants have elevated abortion to the position of a "private right," sterilization (voluntary or not) to the status of a "social benefit," infanticide to the level of pediatric "care," and direct or indirect euthanasia to the place of a "dignity!"

In such times and circumstances, the story of little Margaret of Metola (or Castello) strikes one as being quaint at best—or at worst, hopelessly irrelevant. It is neither, as Father Bonniwell's extensive first-hand research in Italy and the constant—and growing—devotion to Blessed Margaret down through the years prove.

Margaret and her story could not possibly be *more* relevant to these times.

Her parents considered her an embarrassment, and brutally rejected her as "inconvenient," just as tens of millions of parents throughout the world each year reject the children they have conceived as a burden, as "unwanted," and abort them, abandon them, or abuse them to the point of death.

She was shunted aside or regarded as a pious curiosity by the worldly-wise of her day, just as today our society is frightened or made uneasy by physical deformity, and looks for ways of "dealing with" the elderly and infirm that are hardly compassionate or wise.

She was poor, but her "poverty of means" was overcome by the magnanimity and generosity of other poor before it was relieved by the powerful and wealthy.

She was deformed by nature, but only so nature's God could more readily use her as a lesson on what things are (and are not) necessary for "the good life," for a "quality of life"— a life *received* from God, and so shared with Him, first of all, and then with each other.

While reading her story, one is struck by the impression that Margaret is the only "whole" person in it, that those who may be far from the wisdom of the Cross and redemption are really the halt, the lame and the blind!

So it was that eight years ago, while I was giving some theological lectures to the cloistered Dominican Nuns at the Monastery of the Rosary in Summit, New Jersey, they suggested, apropos of my involvement since 1967 in the pro-life movement, that Blessed Margaret of Castello would make an ideal "Patroness of the Unwanted."

I had read an earlier edition of Father Bonniwell's book as a seminarian years before, but until the sisters suggested her importance to our times, the idea had not occurred to me.

Simultaneously, Mrs. Randy Engel, a pro-life colleague and Chairman of the U. S. Coalition for Life, was discussing with me the need for a firmer spiritual base in the lives of pro-life workers and for the movement. It was then that I told her about Margaret of Castello. She was enthusiastic, and immediately began to read, write and speak about Margaret at every opportunity.

It was then that I contacted Father Bonniwell, already into his nineties and himself blind and infirm, and discovered that he had been unsuccessfully attempting to have his biography of Blessed Margaret, by then out-of-print for many years, republished. The publishers told him there was not much of a market for hagiography these days.

"Market" or not, clearly something was happening. After an article by Mrs. Engel about Margaret appeared, she received hundreds of inquiries requesting more information. Simultaneously, more and more Christians, members of pro-life groups or not, have volunteered that they are praying for Blessed Margaret's intercession on behalf of various intentions—especially for a halt to the worldwide holocaust of abortions. And there is evidence that perhaps Margaret is listening and asking the Lord to intervene.

Since IDEA, Inc. published its revised second edition of this book in 1979, thousands of copies have been distributed in the United States, Canada, Ireland, England and Australia. With IDEA's permission, translations from the book into other languages have been made.

Since 1979, new readers of Father Bonniwell's book have again begun to visit Citta di Castello to pray at the tomb containing Margaret's incorrupt remains in the chapel of the School for the Blind conducted by the Dominican Sisters.

During Lent of 1981, *The Irish Catholic,* a weekly newspaper published in Dublin, serialized the book. Recently a cassette recording of Blessed Margaret's story was produced by (and is available from) *Keep the Faith, Inc.,* North Haledon, New Jersey.

Most important to the development of Margaret's cause since our second edition was published was the dedication in April of 1981, by then Archbishop Thomas McDonough of Louisville, Kentucky, of a national shrine honoring Blessed Margaret of Castello. Attached to the Dominican Church of St. Louis Bertrand there, the shrine and the "Blessed Margaret of Castello Crusade" associated with it were the fulfillment of efforts by Fathers Ignatius Cataudo, O.P., Prior, and Father David Moriarty, O.P., Director of the Shrine and Crusade, carried on with the Archbishop's encouragement and help. Their faith and their zeal for Margaret and all the "unwanted of God" were an answered prayer. The Holy Sacrifice of the Mass, together with regular novena services for all Margaret's clients, are powerful evidence of the shrine's dedication to life—and the life of God within us.

Soon after publication of our second edition in 1979, we forwarded a number of copies to the Generalate of the Dominicans at Santa Sabina on the Aventine, in Rome. Specifically, I corresponded with Father Innocenzo Venchi, O.P., General Postulator (Promoter) of Causes for Saints of the Order. He was delighted to learn, apparently for the first time, of the renewed interest in Blessed Margaret since

Father Bonniwell's book was first published in 1952, and has helped us further her cause.

In spring of 1983, Father Timothy Sparks, O.P. (Priory of St. Dominic-St. Thomas, 7200 West Division Street, River Forest, Illinois 60305) was appointed Coordinator for the United States of the Cause of Blessed Margaret of Castello. Father Sparks, formerly a professor of theology and philosophy, and assistant to the Dominican Master General in Rome, is especially well qualified for this role, and his appointment also is evidence of the mounting interest in "the little unwanted Saint" by people in the English-speaking world. Anyone wishing to report cures or other favors granted through the intercession of Blessed Margaret of Castello should write to Father Sparks at River Forest.

Whether in due course, by God's providence, Margaret will allow Father Bonniwell's biography and the efforts of her many clients and friends to prosper, and whether she someday will be canonized and named "Patroness of the Unwanted," no one knows.

One thing is certain. She already has reached into our lives to remind us of the worth God has put there regardless of our circumstances, or, better, precisely by means of them. It is our work, through faith, to understand what God has done. And for now, that is enough. Blessed be God in His angels and in His saints!

> Father Charles Fiore, O.P.
> Chairman, IDEA, Inc.
> Madison, Wisconsin
> April 13, 1983
> Feast of Blessed Margaret of Castello

PRAYER FOR CANONIZATION

Jesus, Mary, Joseph, glorify Thy servant Blessed Margaret, by granting the favor we so ardently desire. This we ask in humble submission to God's Will, for His honor and glory and the salvation of souls. (With Ecclesiastical Approval.)

INTRODUCTION

The story of Margaret of Castello has its setting in Italy on the eve of the Renaissance. At that time Italy was seething in a furious, chaotic turmoil in which the most startling extremes of genius and stupidity, heroism and abject cowardice, contentment and unbridled ambition, humaneness and revolting cruelty appeared side by side in swift succession.

The life-and-death conflict between a way of life deeply rooted in bygone centuries and the new revolutionary ideas that were inflaming the minds of men, the struggle between the old order and the new, nowhere in Europe reached greater intensity or greater depths of savagery than it did in Italy. From Sicily to the Alps, the country was convulsed by an endless series of wars between the Guelphs, who resented foreign domination, and the Ghibellines, who supported the claims of the German emperors. In the grim conflict, not only were Guelphs arrayed against Ghibellines, but cities fought one another, while in every commune the nobility and the lower classes bitterly contended for political power and both parties were invariably split into furious factions.

The ferocity of these quarrels produced such men as Ezzelino da Romano, who inflicted terrible mutilations and horrible deaths upon thousands of men, women, and children; the Visconti tyrants, who by treachery, torture, and bloodshed, tried to gain possession of all Italy; the *condottieri,* who unceasingly marauded the country and by arson, rape, and slaughter, left it a land of desolation. The brutal monsters depicted by Dante in the *Inferno* were not figments of the poet's imagination but real persons who lived in the second half of the thirteenth and the first part of the fourteenth century.

Yet it was in the same atmosphere that the gentle Niccola of Pisa produced his masterpieces in sculpture and in architecture; that Cimabue and his illustrious pupil Giotto,

discarding the old symbolism, introduced naturalism in paint-
ing; that Dante Alighieri, an exile at Ravenna, composed his
immortal *Divina Commedia;* that Petrarch and Boccaccio
enthralled their readers, the one with his sonnets of love, the
other with his satires and stories.

Certainly no biographer could desire a more colorful or
more stirring time and place as a background for his narra-
tive. But great events require great personages, persons
remarkable in the world of art, of literature, or of politics—
or, in the case of a woman, someone noted at least for her
beauty, or for her wit, or even for her crimes. For this very
reason, any biographer of Margaret of Castello works under
a handicap, for Margaret meets none of these requirements.
She committed no crimes; she was not witty; and certainly she
was not beautiful. She composed no sublime poem, painted
no famous picture, and occupied no outstanding position in
politics. She did not even share in any reflected glory by association with the great, nor was she the inspiration for genius,
as Beatrice was for Dante, and Laura for Petrarch.

On the contrary, she was considered so insignificant that
the most detailed histories of medieval Italy do not bother to
mention her. And yet we are confronted with an astonishing
fact: during the course of six hundred years more than
twoscore writers—nearly every one of them men of unusual
education—chancing upon some manuscript that contained
an account of Margaret's life, thought it well worth their
while to publish the story of this obscure girl.

In bringing before the public the almost incredible story of
Margaret of Castello, I am attempting to do tardy justice to
one whose life has been persistently misrepresented by every
writer from the end of the fourteenth century to the present
time. Many historical persons have had their memory injured
by hostile biographers; it has been the singular misfortune of
Margaret to have had her memory consigned almost to oblivi-
on by friendly writers!

Margaret of Castello is first mentioned in *Arbor Vitae* by
the Franciscan, Hubert of Casale (fl. 1325). He was so deeply
impressed by her that he spoke at length of her in his book.

Shortly after her death, an anonymous person wrote her

life. A Canon regular of the Cathedral of Castello branded the book "a tissue of lies." He resolved to expose the "fraud." So he sought out and grilled everyone who had known the girl. Then he searched the archives of the City Hall and of the Cathedral for every official document referring to Margaret. When he finished his long investigation, he had to admit the biographer had told the truth.

But the biography, the Canon tells us, "lacked literary style," so he wrote a new life of Margaret; this one was in Latin. It appeared in 1345. In 1397, a Dominican, shocked by the Canon's poor Latin, rewrote the book in classical Latin. Then, in 1400, another Dominican—Thomas Cafferini—wrote an Italian translation of the book. The first biography disappeared in the 15th century, but the editions of 1345, 1397 and 1400 are still extant. All three were used to compile this book, but whenever I shall speak of "the medieval biographer," it is the Canon to whom I refer, as he is the chief source of our knowledge of Margaret.

The Canon's manuscript reveals that he was writing only for his own fellow-citizens, and indeed, for those of his own day. He says in his conclusion that "many other things could be truthfully told about Margaret." But he omits them because, as he declares, "Everybody is still talking about them!" So what is the use of recording what everybody already knows?

Pursuant to this strange reasoning, he tells us nothing of contemporary political issues, local customs, the harsh laws concerning crime, or of the horrors of a medieval prison. Yet all these factors affected Margaret's life—some of them to a drastic degree.

Fortunately, there still exist a number of 14th and 15th century manuscripts which give the history of the various republics involved, as well as biographies of personages of that era, legal documents, correspondence of officials, etc. These documents supply us with much of the data which the Canon of Castello omitted.

A late source of information is a long report published in 1600. The preceding year, St. Robert Bellarmine—the most erudite scholar of that time—undertook a thorough investigation of the subject of Margaret of Castello. His report is valuable for several reasons, one of which is that he quotes extensively from old documents which later perished during the Napoleonic Wars in Italy.

The family name of Margaret was concealed by the 14th century biographers and today is still uncertain. Because of this, she is variously called "Margaret of Metola," her birthplace, and "Margaret of Castello," where she died. Actually, there is no town in Italy named simply "Castello"—the town referred to is "Citta di Castello." But English writers shorten the name to "Castello," just as they shorten "Massa Trabaria" to "Trabaria."

In conclusion, I wish to express my gratitude to the many persons in Citta di Castello for their unstinted efforts to assist me in my researches every time I visited their city. In the region once called Massa Trabaria (Mercatello, Metola, Sant'Angelo in Vado, etc.), the eager cooperation given me resulted in unearthing valuable data not given by the medieval biographers.

To all my Italian "assistants"—my deepest and warmest thanks!

Fr. William R. Bonniwell, O.P.
April 13, 1979

Chapter I

THE CASTLE OF METOLA

In the Apennine Mountains, in a lonely, obscure part of Italy just southeast of the republic of Florence, there was in the thirteenth and fourteenth centuries a Papal State named Massa Trabaria. It comprised only about 300 square miles, yet—despite its smallness—it was coveted by its powerful neighbors, Florence, Urbino, Arezzo and Perugia, both because of its strategic position and because of its valuable forests.

Anyone travelling today through this country and observing how sparse and small the trees are, finds it difficult to believe that centuries ago these mountains were famous for their mighty forests. It was here that in ancient times the Romans obtained much of their timber, floating the huge logs down the nearby Tiber from Bocca Trabaria to Rome. Even in the Middle Ages the great woods of Massa Trabaria continued to furnish the lumber needed for the buildings of the Eternal City.

At the beginning of the thirteenth century, Pope Innocent III reorganized the Papal States from Rome to Ravenna. As Massa Trabaria lay in the center of the States, its military security became a matter of vital importance. For this reason the Pope raised the province to the dignity of a commonwealth, and ordered it to be strongly fortified. The little republic so organized managed to preserve its autonomy until 1443, when it was "absorbed" by the Duchy of Urbino.

The success of Massa Trabaria in resisting for more than two centuries the invasions of powerful neighbors was largely due to its fortifications, the warlike spirit of the mountaineers, and the wild, rough nature of the terrain. The entire country was not only ruggedly mountainous but also heavily wooded. The few rivers that took their rise there were too small to be navigable, and the roads were infrequent and primitive. As a result, the rural districts were sparsely settled.

1

Anyone leaving Sant'Angelo in Vado by the southwest road was confronted by an arresting sight almost as soon as he was beyond the city gates. For there two long valleys converged toward him. The valley on his right was quite level and stretched to the west, to the town of Mercatello; the other, which opened directly in front of him, steadily climbed higher and higher in a straight line until its course was abruptly checked by a high mountain squarely blocking its path. Perched on the lofty crest of this mountain like a watchful eagle, and standing out boldly against the blue Italian sky, was a strong fortress, the castle of Metola.

Even in those days the castle was not without a certain amount of mystery, for no one knew the date it was erected or who built it. But this much is certain: it was built before the beginning of the thirteenth century—as we find it mentioned in a Vatican document written in the twelfth century. Probably local tradition is correct in stating that the castle was built as a defense against the Saracens, whose repeated invasions plagued central Italy during the eleventh and twelfth centuries. The unknown builder, in choosing this spot, had displayed sound judgment. Not only did the castle dominate the surrounding country, but, even with the mountains covered by great forests, it also had a good view of the important highway between the two principal towns of Massa Trabaria. Had the traveller scaled the steep mountain and drawn closer to the fort, he would have seen that the mountaintop had been so skillfully utilized for defense that the castle was well-nigh impregnable; three sides were protected by precipitous slopes, while the fourth side—the only one at all accessible—was guarded by a wide, deep moat.

The frequent attempts by neighboring republics to capture the castle of Metola attest to its strategic importance. One of these efforts, made by the Republic of Gubbio at the middle of the thirteenth century, was successful through treachery, and possession of the fort remained in their hands for nearly a quarter of a century. The State Council of Massa Trabaria, on the death of their aged Captain of the People, selected his son, a young officer named Parisio, as his successor.

The new commander proved himself to be a fearless and

capable soldier. One of his first acts was to lead his army up the heights of Metola and lay siege to the fortress. Although at that period the means of military defense were far superior to those of attack, such was Parisio's military genius that he successfully stormed the fortress.

The regaining of this stronghold, which was in the heart of the southern half of Massa Trabaria, made Parisio a national hero. The enthusiastic natives, in gratitude, bestowed upon their victorious leader the fortress and the extensive estate of which it was part. It was to this mountain stronghold that Parisio brought his young bride, Emilia. This noble couple possess for us a special interest, because they occupy a prominent place in our story. Unfortunately, the medieval biographer fails to describe for us the appearance of either the noble lord or his lady.

There was something else he failed to record (but this failure was not due to negligence, only to a sense of discretion)—the family names of the husband and wife. Parisio was the man's first or given name, just as Emilia was the Christian name of his wife. Without the slightest shadow of a doubt, the surnames of both persons were known to the medieval biographer. But in those days of violence, when noblemen so often placed themselves above the law, it would have been exceedingly rash to have stamped with infamy a powerful house intensely proud of its family honor. Since those days, scholars have repeatedly searched the most likely archives in an effort to discover Parisio's surname, but without success.

The biographer does tell us, however, of the social and political prominence of Parisio. He was much more than just another nobleman. The fact that not only he, but a number of his ancestors, held the post of Captain of the People, proves the political importance of the family. The government of Massa Trabaria, like that of many republics of the Middle Ages, sought a balance of power by dividing the functions of government between a *podesta*, a Captain of the People, and a State Council. The *podesta*, with the help of the Council, ruled within the capital city; but it was the Captain of the People who exercised authority over the rest of the land, and who, in time of war, became commander in chief of the armies.

Besides being politically important, Parisio was also a wealthy man. In addition to his family inheritance, and his salary as one of the highest officials of the land, he became, after his victory at Metola, the castellan of a powerful fortress, where he enjoyed the revenues of a large and valuable seigniory. The forests alone on his estate were of enormous value; but over and above that, his income was augmented by the forced labor extracted from the hapless serfs by their seignior and by the taxes and fees they had to pay him. The many proofs of Parisio's wealth are confirmed by the testimony of a contemporary Franciscan, Hubert of Casale, who knew Margaret well and who testified that she came "from a noble wealthy family."

Parisio was apparently endowed with few virtues. He was monstrously proud, unscrupulous, and indifferent to the sufferings of others. He was merciless toward anyone who stood in his way. Wholly selfish and engrossed in himself, he was not capable of genuine affection toward anyone, except insofar as that individual might be of some value to him. He did not believe that God—if there were a God—took any interest whatever in human beings and their actions.

Of his wife, Lady Emilia, less is known. She seems to have been a woman of weak character, completely and abjectly under the domination of her husband. After examining her life, the medieval biographer can find only two praiseworthy things to say about her: she had her child baptized, and she occasionally visited it!

Such were the characters of the castellan Parisio and his wife Emilia. Undoubtedly, had this couple died childless, their very existence would have long since been forgotten by mankind, as it has forgotten the existence of tens of thousands of other lords and ladies. But in the beginning of the year 1287 it had become common knowledge in and about the castle of Metola that before the end of the year Lady Emilia would give birth to a child.

At the prospect of having a son to perpetuate his name, Parisio was overjoyed. So important an event had to be celebrated in a becoming manner.

"*Cara mia,*" he said to his wife, "I have been thinking about the banquet in honor of our first-born. You know, some of our friends, especially the elderly ones, would have quite a hard time climbing this mountain, and besides, we do not have enough guest rooms for everybody. So why don't we have two banquets: one here, for the garrison and the serfs; then a few weeks later, at our house in Mercatello, we could have an elaborate banquet for all our friends."

"Oh, that is a wonderful idea!" exclaimed his wife. "And the banquet in town would serve for both the baby's birth and his baptism."

His baptism! Parisio had not given that a thought! Yet, if his enemies informed Rome that he, a Captain of the People in a Papal State, had failed to have his child baptized, it could easily mean the ruin of his plans. It was clever of his wife to have thought of that!

Emilia went on: "We may just as well draw up now the list of guests and give it to the seneschal, so that he can get the invitations ready. You had better instruct him to begin his preparations right away."

When the seneschal studied the list, his eyes widened. Not only were all the important people of Massa Trabaria to be invited, but even a number of dignitaries from neighboring states. He began to realize that it would not be easy to carry out Parisio's order: "I want you to prepare the best feast ever given in Massa Trabaria. Do not dishonor my name by stinting in anything."

The feast at the castle would give the seneschal no trouble. Only the soldiers, the civilians in the fort, and the serfs on the estate would partake of it. For them, it would be enough to provide plenty of wine and an abundance of venison, pigs, ducks, rabbits and pastries. But the affair at Mercatello would require the very best!

Although Parisio's wine cellar in town was well stocked, the seneschal thought it prudent to send a purveyor to Florence to purchase a tun (a medieval measure) of the very best wine procurable, to engage first-class minstrels and entertainers (without whom no feast could be a success), and to buy several peacocks, to be served after the various meats. The peacocks would be a fitting climax! As he reviewed his menu, the seneschal smiled contentedly; the feast would indeed be worthy of the first-born son of Parisio! His castellan need have no worry!

As a matter of fact, the castellan was not worrying. His mind was dwelling on the more distant future—the career his son would have in Italian politics. Ezzelino da Romano had shown what a soldier who feared neither God nor man could accomplish! A kingdom was to be had at the expense of the weaker Papal States, and Parisio determined he would lay the foundations of such a kingdom for his son.

Everything he saw spoke to him of his dreams. One day he happened to pass the armorer's forge. He watched the skill of the armorer who was repairing a shield.

"It won't be many years now, Paolo, before you'll be making a suit of armor for my son, eh?" he remarked.

"Your Excellency, I'll make him the finest suit of armor in all Italy!" boasted the armorer.

Indeed everybody at Metola, including the half-starved serfs, who lived scattered throughout the forests, shared wholeheartedly the anticipation of their liege lord, but from very different motives. The birth of an heir meant not only an abundance of good food for several days, but also largesse from the Captain, and even music and entertainment! It was therefore with much hope that, day after day, the serfs paused in their task of felling trees in the heart of the forest and listened for the great bell of the castle to peal forth its joyous message to the countryside.

But the day on which the child was born, the castle bell remained silent; no flag fluttered proudly from the high tower; no herald on gaily-caparisoned horse thundered across the drawbridge to proclaim the news. There was no banquet, no entertainment, no largesse. That night, instead of a castle ablaze with lights and resounding with noisy festivities, all was darkness and silence. Silence and darkness were more suited to the despair and horror that crushed the hearts of Parisio and the Lady Emilia.

The child was a girl. And the girl was dreadfully deformed.

Chapter II

THE DAUGHTER OF THE CASTELLAN

The birth of a deformed child is always a great shock to the parents. But usually the very misfortune of the infant touches the hearts of the father and mother so deeply that, by reason of their compassion, they lavish greater love on the cripple than they do on their normal children—but Parisio and Emilia were not of that type. Their fantastic pride and selfishness rendered them incapable of pity, and they looked upon their deformed baby with anger and loathing. They were outraged that Nature should have even dared to inflict so shameful a disgrace upon the two most important personages of the land!

From a purely materialistic standpoint, Margaret's parents were not without some excuse for their attitude, because Nature, as if she were acting in a malicious mood, had heaped one misfortune after another upon the unhappy child. Margaret was far from being beautiful, but her ugliness was the least of her handicaps. She was so small that it was evident she would never attain normal height. In addition, she was hunchbacked. As the right leg was much shorter than the left, it was obvious that the girl would be lame. All this was bad enough. But a week or so after her birth, her parents discovered that she had still another handicap. She was totally blind.

When the parents had recovered from the initial shock, they agreed that their misfortune should be kept a profound secret. Of course, the birth of a child could not be concealed, but the news was given out that the baby was sickly and was not likely to live. This accounted to friends for the absence of any celebration and explained at the same time the obvious grief of the parents.

To the garrison, however, it was bluntly stated that silence concerning the child would be very prudent; the remembrance of the revolting cruelties inflicted by Parisio on some of his prisoners made the warning effective. The serving-woman who had the care and custody of the baby was under strict orders to keep the child out of sight whenever any visitors came to Metola

Despite these precautions, the first threat to the secret came from within the castle itself. Padre Cappellano, who was apparently both pastor of the parish of Metola and the chaplain of the fort, demanded that the baby be baptized. This meant, in effect, that the child should be taken to the cathedral in Mercatello, because there still existed in Massa Trabaria the ancient custom whereby all baptisms (except in urgent cases) were performed in the cathedral church of the diocese.

Parisio stubbornly refused to run this risk, and it was not until the priest had won over Lady Emilia that the castellan gave a reluctant consent. Lady Emilia's discreet and trustworthy maid was to take the baby to Mercatello. The name to be given her in baptism was a matter of indifference to her parents—except that she was *not* to receive the name Emilia.

It was, then, the maid who chose the name Margaret. In so doing she surely did not reflect on the meaning of the word, for *Margarita* means a pearl. And what comparison could there possibly be between this ugly, misshapen baby and the lovely pearl—that symbol of perfection and beauty?

One might imagine that with the passing of the years the harsh feelings of the parents would soften and they would begin to show at least a little commiseration for their crippled daughter. Such, however, was not the case. Time crystallized, if it did not intensify, their abhorrence for the child. It was in vain that the chaplain, who had begun to teach her the rudiments of religion, repeatedly told the parents of the remarkable intelligence their daughter was beginning to manifest; his enthusiasm left them cold and uninterested.

By the time she was five years old, Margaret knew the name of every man, woman and child at Metola. She could make her way unassisted through the various passageways of the fort and the corridors of every building. As she was a friendly little creature, she made regular visits to everyone. There was only one place that she carefully avoided: it was the quarters where her parents lived. She had been emphatically warned to stay away from this part of the castle, as her parents did not want to see her.

But the very friendliness of Margaret was fated to bring her new suffering. One day, when she was six years old, visitors came to Metola, but through forgetfulness, the nurse failed to warn Margaret to stay in her room. The child, in accordance with her custom, went to the chapel to pray. On her way, she met one of the women visitors, who was moved with pity at the sight of the cripple.

"Are you blind, little girl?"

"Yes, Your Ladyship."

The visitor was astonished.

"If you cannot see, how do you know I am a lady?"

"Because you do not speak like the wives of the soldiers. Your voice is like that of my mother or of Lady Gemma."

The lady's astonishment grew greater.

"Your mother? What is your mother's name, dear?"

Before the child could answer, there came running down the corridor a large, fat peasant woman, who almost rudely thrust herself between the lady and the child.

"Excuse me, Your Ladyship," she panted, "but this little girl is ill and should have remained in her room. You naughty child! Go back to your room at once!" And loudly scolding her, she rushed Margaret down the corridor.

When Parisio and Emilia learned of the incident, they were aghast at the narrowness of their escape. They shuddered at the thought of the news being bruited throughout Massa Trabaria that the lord and lady of Metola had a shockingly deformed daughter. It was obvious that if they allowed Margaret to continue to enjoy the freedom of the fort, they would be courting eventual discovery.

Something had to be done, but what? Emilia suggested finding some peasant, farther back in the mountain, who would rear the child. Parisio dismissed the idea as presenting too many difficulties. A silence ensued, during which the castellan took to walking up and down the room. Of a sudden he stopped.

"Emilia! What was that silly story the chaplain was telling

you at dinner yesterday? I was not paying much attention to him."

"What silly story do you mean?"

"Don't you remember? Something about a crazy woman who shut herself up in a prison some place near Florence."

"You mean St. Veridiana?"

"That's the name! What was the story?"

Emilia gazed wide-eyed at her husband. Was he jesting or did he actually want to hear a pious story?

"Well?" said Parisio irritably. "Don't you remember?"

Emilia, still unable to believe her ears, mechanically began.

"The chaplain said that this saint wanted to do penance, so she had a small cell built next to a church."

She paused uncertainly, but it was evident that Parisio wanted her to continue.

"The cell had a tiny window through the church wall," she continued, "so that the recluse could see the altar and attend Mass, but could not be seen by the congregation. On the other side of the cell there was another small window, through which food was passed in to the saint. This second window had a black curtain hung in front of it so that no one could see the saint. The chaplain said that she lived there for more than thirty years and that on one occasion St. Francis of Assisi—"

"Never mind the rest!" interrupted Parisio testily. He resumed his walking up and down the room. Finally, he turned to his wife and said slowly, "Do you know, I think our chaplain has solved the problem for us."

'But I don't see—" began the bewildered Emilia.

"Look, you told me that Margaret is very devout, that she likes to spend hours in the chapel praying. Good! We'll make her happy by allowing her to pray all day long in church."

One look at Emilia's face made it obvious that she had no idea of what her husband meant. Parisio now stood in front of her and spoke patiently, as if explaining something elementary to a child.

"My good wife, we will build a small cell next to the

church, just like that St.—what did you call her?—Veridiana. Then we'll install Margaret in the cell and make a recluse out of her."

"But, Parisio," gasped his wife, "you cannot shut her up in a prison like that. She is a mere child; she is only six years old. The Church won't permit a child to become a recluse."

"The Church has nothing to do with this. This is a private family matter. You can explain to Margaret what a great privilege we are going to bestow on her; she'll be able to pray from morning to night without anyone disturbing her! Besides, it will be for her own good, it will keep her out of danger. Wandering around the fort the way she does, she might get badly hurt. In the cell, she will be safe. And there will be no danger of any visitors seeing her! Tomorrow I'll order the mason to build the cell!"

The church to which Parisio was referring was not the chapel of the castle (where such a cell would be noticed by visitors), but a little church in the forest, about a quarter of a mile away; it was called the Church of St. Mary of the Fortress of Metola. It was the parish church of the whole area known as Metola. It was ideally suited to Parisio's plan, because the ruggedness of the mountain would effectually discourage any guests at the castle from visiting it.

Since the structure planned by Parisio was a small, low-ceilinged affair, it took the mason only a few days to build it. Then the castellan, with scant ceremony, thrust the child into the prison and ordered the mason to wall up the doorway.

Never again would the little cripple play with other children in the warm sunlight: henceforth, she was to be separated from the rest of mankind, as if she were a vicious criminal or a dangerous leper. For it was the intention of her father that she should remain immured there until death came to set her free. After all, a prominent nobleman like Parisio could not permit his family honor to become sullied!

Chapter III

THE PRISONER

On the day Margaret was imprisoned, life outwardly went on as usual at the fort. Apparently no one saw anything and certainly no one said anything; to have done so would not have been prudent. But in the privacy of their quarters the soldiers and their wives carried on much angry whispering.

Nowhere was the whispering more emphatic and prolonged that evening than in the chambers of the knight Leonardo di Peneto, who was second in command of the castle. After supper, as soon as the servants had departed, the knight bolted and barred the outer door, and then crossed the room to take a seat beside his wife, Lady Gemma, who was sitting in front of the fireplace.

"Oh, Leonardo!" she exclaimed, with tears in her eyes. "Think of that poor, unfortunate child out there all alone in the forest and shivering in her cold prison! It's horrible! Horrible!"

"Yes, it is horrible enough," replied her husband sadly, for he was fond of the child. "The men of the garrison are in a rage about it."

"They are in a rage," repeated Gemma scornfully, "but with the exception of yourself trying to dissuade Parisio, they did not dare speak up in her behalf!"

"One man did. I heard him."

"Who? What did he say?" eagerly demanded Gemma.

The knight lowered his voice still more.

"This afternoon I was at my post on the walls when Padre Cappellano got back from his trip to Milan. He had been in the fort only a short time when he shot by me like an arrow and sped into the great hall of the castle. It wasn't long before I heard him and the castellan shouting at each other."

"That timid mouse?" asked Gemma incredulously. "He would not dare shout at Parisio!"

"Your timid mouse, Gemma, told Parisio to his face that he

13

was lower than a beast to imprison his daughter, and he demanded that the girl be released at once!"

Gemma was bewildered. "I simply cannot believe it! The Padre has always been such a timorous little man!"

"But wait! The worst is yet to come. Parisio bellowed that Margaret would remain where she was, and he added, 'If you don't mind your own business, I'll rip the tongue out of your head!' I thought that threat would silence the Padre. Instead, he invoked the wrath of God upon both Parisio and his wife!"

Gemma grew white and hastily made the Sign of the Cross. It seemed to her that some terrible malignant presence had taken possession of the castle, and for a while her lips moved in silent prayer. Then, in a low voice, she said:

"Leonardo, I am worried about Margaret. To be cast out like that—to know that her parents despise her—. And she is not strong; if she has to stay in that wretched, damp cell, I am afraid her health will give way."

"I am more concerned about her mind than about her health. It would have been better for her to have been subnormal mentally as well as physically."

"Leonardo!" remonstrated his wife. "How can you say a thing like that!"

"If her mind were not developed, Gemma, she would not be too sensitive to pain. But, as you know, she has an extraordinary intelligence; that means she will suffer all the more from physical pain—not to mention how her heart must ache for her parents' love. . . . It also means that, as she gets older, she will suffer intensely from the knowledge of what she is being deprived of in life!"

"Perhaps she already knows that," hinted his wife.

"No, dear, she does not. I once knew a blind woman who told me that when she was little she thought all children were blind like herself. She was twelve years old before she learned the truth."

"I was not going to tell you this, Leonardo, but Margaret already knows she is abnormal," Gemma interposed resolutely.

"But that is not possible. What makes you think so?"

"One day I kissed her and told her how much I loved her.

She asked me, wondering, 'But how can you? My babbo and mamma told me no one could love me because I am a freak!' "

"Gemma! That is incredible!"

"I am telling you just what the child said. Margaret then asked what was a freak, and they told her that other children were not blind, or midgets, or lame, or hunchbacked; that she was all these things, and, to top it all, she was as ugly as sin!"

The soldier grew white with rage. In a loud, angry voice he cried:

"The vile, contemptible curs! Why doesn't God strike them dead?"

Gemma, terrified, clapped her hand over his mouth.

"Hush, dear! Hush! Suppose someone should hear you!"

As if in response to her warning, there came an insistent rapping at the door. The knight arose and strode across the room. He unbarred and opened the door.

"Oh!" he exclaimed in relief. "It is you, Padre. Come in."

As the priest entered, he remarked with a faint smile, "I heard loud talking, so I knew you had not yet gone to bed." As Leonardo rebarred the door, the priest placed his lantern on a bench and crossed the room to a seat near the hearth. The knight sat beside him and said in a low voice:

"We are speaking about little Margaret." The priest nodded. "Tell me, Father," continued the soldier, "did you know that her parents have revealed to her how much she differs from a normal child?"

"Yes, I have known it for some time," was the quiet reply.

"They would have shown more mercy," muttered the knight, "if they had cut the child's throat!"

"Father, what is going to become of the poor creature?" asked Lady Gemma. "Her afflictions cut her off from the rest of her fellow beings even more than her prison walls do. She knows that she can never live the normal life of a woman. She will not be able to marry and have a home of her own. She knows that she is not wanted. What a horrible future lies before her! Mark my words, Father, one day that unhappy girl will go insane."

"That is very likely," agreed her husband. "Either she will

lose her mind, or, if she lives, she will become a bitterly
unhappy creature, hating herself and every human being."

"I know I should not say it," cried Lady Gemma, bursting
into tears, "but it would be better that the unhappy child die
and be released from her misery."

A silence ensued. The chaplain waited a while until he was
sure that the emotion of Leonardo and his lady had expended
itself. Then he began to speak in his timid, apologetic voice.

"Isn't it strange how few of us Christians really put into
practice what our Faith teaches us?"

"Why, what do you mean—put into practice—?"

"Well," replied the priest, "our Faith teaches that God created us to love Him, and in that love to find eternal and perfect happiness. My greatest aim then, in a life filled with all
kinds of obstacles and distractions, should be to develop to
the highest degree my love of God. To do this, I do not need
eyesight, or a normal body, or the love and affection of my
fellow man—agreeable and pleasant as all these things are."

The priest was staring at the burning logs of the hearth and
seemed to be speaking to himself, rather than to his friends.

"Now, little Margaret understands this very clearly. And
she also knows that one of the most efficacious ways in which
love can be deepened, strengthened, purified, is by suffering.
Our Savior taught us that the royal road to perfect love is the
Cross. Everyone has noticed how contented and cheerful
Margaret has always been; the reason is that she regards her
handicaps and deformities as being merely the means
whereby she can more surely reach her God."

The priest turned to the knight's wife.

"Lady Gemma, a moment ago you said that it would be
better for the child to die. You are wrong. It is better, a thou-
sand times better, both for herself and for countless others,
that she should live."

"But, Father," protested Gemma, "think of all the
pleasures she will miss in life, and of all the sufferings she will
have to undergo!"

"My child, God is well worth any price that we can pay. I
grant you that a heavy burden has been laid on young
shoulders; but Margaret has been given a keen mind—a

luminous mind—with which she clearly apprehends the issue at stake. Furthermore, she has received the graces necessary to carry her cross. If she does not falter, a glorious victory will one day be hers; yes, the time will come when she will bless the day she was born blind and deformed. Let us, her friends, pray as we have never prayed before, that her faith and courage fail her not!"

The soldier made an impatient move.

"Father, you are expecting a mere child to act like a St. Francis or a St. Anthony! Be reasonable!"

"Messer Leonardo," replied the priest, "this afternoon, when I returned from my trip, I had hardly reached my rooms when I had a number of visitors; they came to inform me of what Parisio had done. They all remarked how brave Margaret had been, that she did not shed a tear. After my interview with Parisio, I went down to see little Margaret. She was sobbing as if her heart were broken."

"Naturally!" cried the knight. "That is just what I am contending. You are expecting too much from a child."

"But do you know why she was crying?" persisted the priest.

"Surely the answer is obvious, isn't it? It is a frightful blow to a child so deeply affectionate as Margaret to be imprisoned by her own parents!"

"Yes," agreed the chaplain. "For her, it was pure agony. And I thought that was why she was weeping. But she soon disillusioned me."

The priest's voice had suddenly become unsteady. To conceal his emotion he rose from his seat, and placing a hand on the shoulder of the knight, he continued:

"As well as I know Margaret, her reply left me shaken. She said, 'Father, when they brought me here this morning, I did not understand—because of my sins—why God let this happen to me. But now He has made it clear. Jesus was rejected even by His own people, and God is letting me be treated the same so that I can follow Our dear Lord more closely. And oh! Father, I am not good enough to be so near to God!"

"And she was so overcome by the thought of God's love for her that she could not continue. ... Well—good night, dear friends. May God bless you and keep you!"

Hastily he crossed the room. In silence Leonardo unbarred the door for him, and the priest, his lantern in hand, made his way along the dark corridor.

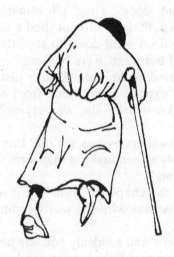

Chapter IV

MARGARET'S SUFFERING

In describing the blind girl's mind as "luminous," the chaplain had used the right word. Margaret's understanding of life and its problems was truly extraordinary. This was partly due to the instruction given her by the patient chaplain. But there can be no question that it was, in a far greater degree, due to divine grace. We are irresistibly reminded of a like early development of intelligence in St. Catherine of Siena, St. Catherine de Ricci, and St. Rose of Lima, when they were the same age. The course of instruction she received was so thorough, and so completely absorbed by Margaret, that years later she astonished the Dominican friars at Citta di Castello with the extent and depth of her theological knowledge.

With Margaret, to know was to act. She possessed so generous a nature that she felt she had given nothing to God so long as anything remained to be given. With her, therefore, there could never be any question of compromise or of half measures. Since she had chosen to serve God, she would do so with her whole heart, her whole soul and her whole mind.

"It isn't the body that is important, Margaret," cried the chaplain. "It makes little difference what sort of a body you have, because in a few short years it will crumble away to the dust. The thing that counts is your soul; that lives forever. God created it to His own image and likeness. Just think, Margaret! God is your real Father. He tenderly loves you and He asks you to love Him in return!"

The teaching of the chaplain filled the child with joy and hope. It safeguarded her disposition against the cruel jibes of her parents concerning her physical appearance. It fired her with determination to do everything she could in order to make herself worthy of such divine love.

The example of the Savior in undergoing voluntarily the greatest suffering for the salvation of the human race made a profound impression on Margaret. She often reflected on the subject, and she began to comprehend what the Savior was trying to teach pleasure-loving mankind. She understood more and more the immensity of God's love which impelled Him to go to such extremes in order to save His children from their folly.

There was nothing morbid in Margaret's character. She had a sunny, cheerful disposition, and she naturally shrank from pain and suffering. But she knew that to grow in virtue and thus approach closer and closer to God, the road she must travel along was the road pointed out by her Savior. As she wanted God more than anything in the whole universe, she was resolved to accept the divine invitation and follow her Savior even to Calvary. Hence, although the action of her parents was an agonizing blow to her, Margaret realized that God had permitted this to happen for her own good, and she forced her reluctant human nature to accept the blow as a special gift from God.

More than ever, she neglected nothing whatever which could help her gain her objective. She not only accepted the sufferings inflicted upon her, but she even sought suffering. Thus, she bound herself at the age of seven to a strict monastic fast—a fast extending from the middle of September (the Feast of the Holy Cross) to the following Easter.

But this was not penance enough for the young, ardent lover of God. She devised a fast of her own to cover the rest of the year, that is, from Easter until the middle of September; during this period she fasted four days a week. On all Fridays of the year, the only nourishment she would accept was a little bread and water.

Still she was not satisfied that she was doing enough. She somehow secretly obtained a hairshirt and began to wear the penitential garment before she was seven years old. Her medieval biographer mentions Margaret's fears that her mother, on her infrequent visits, might notice the bulkiness of the child's dress and grow suspicious. But Lady Emilia was too deeply preoccupied with her misfortune as the mother of a creature like Margaret to pay close attention to the child. So Margaret's secret remained undiscovered.

Meanwhile, the years were slowly passing by, but the prisoner kept no track of them. What she did take notice of was the succession of the seasons. Spring she always welcomed, for she suffered cruelly from the intense cold; but the pleasure of spring was soon ended by the stifling heat of summer, and the relief given by autumn warned her to prepare for another numbing winter.

As she neared teenage, she learned to her dismay that nature, which already had treated her so harshly, had yet another misery in store for her. As if to deride the ugly, deformed girl, nature gave her a passionate disposition which would be a constantly recurring torture to her. For Margaret, to be virtuous was not easy; all her life she would have to struggle, and struggle hard, to remain so.

She had spent 12 years in prison, when the passing of time revealed the first of three events that would drastically affect her, even though the persons involved in these events never even heard of her.

At Perugia, on June 5, 1305, a French Cardinal was elected Pope. Since bitter warfare between political factions was still going on in Rome, the only way the newly-elected Pope, Clement V, could enter that city would be with an army. He preferred to go to France, and he was crowned at Lyons on November 14. The people of Massa Trabaria had always been staunch in their loyalty to the Pope, but this election worried them. If Trabaria were attacked, would a French Pope try to save the little republic? The longer Clement V tarried in France, the greater became their uneasiness.

The same question was being asked in the State Council of Urbino. The ruler of Urbino was Frederic of Montefeltro, one of the ablest generals in central Italy.

The Council concluded that a French Pope would not intervene if Trabaria were attacked. The danger of any state coming to its aid could be avoided by a surprise invasion which would crush the little republic in ten or twelve days. Before any state could mobilize, the war would be over. Accordingly, it was decided that in the spring, Montefeltro would invade.

Meanwhile, in her prison at Metola, Margaret knew

nothing of the gathering storm which in a few months would sweep over her country and remove her from Metola forever.

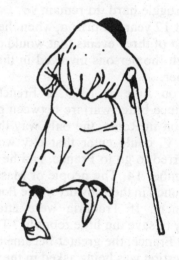

Chapter V

MARGARET EXCHANGES PRISONS

One morning during her 13th year in prison, Margaret realized with a start that it was now some time since the wintry winds had been howling and screaming through the snow-laden trees of the forest; their place had been taken by soft, gentle breezes. She became conscious of the excited gurgling of the mountain freshets created by the melting snow, and she inhaled the fragrant aroma of the pine trees which came stealing into her cell, as if to share in her imprisonment. But above all, it was the lusty singing of countless thrushes which filled her heart to overflowing, for the birds seemed to be telling her how they hurried back from the south, as soon as the weather permitted, to be with their little blind friend.

To Margaret it was God who was talking to her through the many voices of nature, and she was deeply moved by these delicate attentions of her Divine Lover. But this particular year the annual miracle of nature's reawakening to life was destined to bring pleasure to Margaret for only a brief time. Indeed, not many weeks had passed since the return of the birds when abruptly the warning came that new sufferings were at hand.

At first it was very faint. Even the blind girl, who relied so much on her sense of hearing, could catch it only when the wind was right. It sounded as if it were the town bell of Sant'Angelo in Vado, far to the north; but if so, why was it ringing so soon after Terce? A vague uneasiness crept into Margaret's thoughts.

The meaning of the bell was soon made clear. The sharp eyes of the watchman in the castle of Metola saw smoke rising in the distance from burning farmhouses toward the border of Massa Trabaria; he shouted down to Messer Leonardo what he saw, and the next moment the huge castle bell began to shriek its message: Massa Trabaria was being invaded! To arms!

To the trembling prisoner it seemed as if the frenzied bell would never stop its harsh refrain. Tears came to her eyes as she thought of all the sin and misery that invariably accompanied war; then a thought blazed into her mind which filled her with cold horror. Her father! He was Captain of the People! It would be his duty to lead the Massa Trabarians against the invaders! He might be taken prisoner, or wounded, or killed! The frightened girl fell to her knees, and with tears streaming down her cheeks, earnestly implored God to save her country from its enemies, and to watch over the safety of her father.

The alarm given by Messer Leonardo had hardly ended when a courier arrived from the State Council informing Parisio that the land was being invaded by Montefeltro of Urbino. The castle was already a scene of feverish preparations. Parisio, now in full authority as supreme commander, was sending messengers throughout the land to call all serfs to report at once for feudal military duty. Anyone who refused this call was to be forthwith hanged as a warning to others. The younger soldiers of the garrison at Metola were notified to get ready for immediate departure; the older soldiers would remain to guard the castle.

While Parisio's squire was helping him to don his hauberk and fasten the sword to his belt, the Captain continued to issue orders. The storehouse in the bailey was to be opened and weapons were to be distributed to the serfs as they arrived. The seneschal was to search the nearby mountains and seize all the grain and livestock from the farmers for the army.

As soon as all necessary orders had been issued, the Captain hurried to his wife's apartment. He found her standing at the arched window, gazing apprehensively at the distant, ominous columns of smoke.

"Is the situation very serious?" she asked anxiously.

"Yes. Montefeltro has crossed the eastern border with a strong force. You had better pack what you need and go to Mercatello as soon as possible."

"Are you going to abandon the fort, Parisio?"

"No, but I am obliged to take the best soldiers. I want you

to go to Mercatello; it is well fortified and strongly gar-
risoned. You'll be much safer there."

Lady Emilia's eyes lighted up with joy. Life at Mercatello
would be far more pleasant than at the fortress. She turned to
summon her waiting-maid, when a thought struck her.

"Parisio! What about Margaret?"

"You will have to take the little freak with you," the
castellan answered impatiently. "We cannot leave her here, as
enemy patrols will be scouting through the forests and they
would find her."

"But it will be impossible to conceal her in Mercatello! Our
house will be overrun with visitors!"

"Have you forgotten that there are vaults under the
palazzo? Lock her up in one of those."

"But she will want to attend Mass and receive the Sacraments."

Parisio exploded. His nerves were on edge at the thought
that he would be facing on the battlefield one of the ablest
military leaders of the day. He exclaimed angrily:

"Then take your dear daughter to the town piazza at high
noon and introduce her to everybody! You may as well do
that as to allow the garrulous old rector of the cathedral to
learn of her existence. She is not to leave the underground
vaults and she is to have no visitors."

Parisio strode out of the room and hurried to the courtyard
where the soldiers were awaiting him. Placing himself at their
head, he rode out of the castle. The next morning, Lady
Emilia and her attendants left the castle and took with them a
small, heavily-veiled girl.

After thirteen years of imprisonment, Margaret left her
cell, but she would soon learn that she was being transferred
to another prison. When the party reached Mercatello, Lady
Emilia had her daughter quickly led down the stone steps of
the *palazzo* to an underground vault, which had been hastily
prepared for the girl. The furnishings consisted of a miserable pallet and an old bench. There was no other furniture in
the vault.

Then, as if to conform to the custom in most jails, she was
briefed on the regulations of her new prison. Food would be

brought to her twice a day; if there was anything she wanted, she was to wait until mealtime to state her wants. Under no circumstances was she to call out; at all times she was to preserve absolute quiet. When the rules had been stated, the heavy wooden door of the vault was slammed shut, the bolts were shot into their sockets, and Margaret once more found herself alone.

Here at Mercatello, Margaret suffered more intensely than ever before. During her long captivity at Metola she had been sustained by the consolations and helps of her religion—Mass, the sacraments of Penance and Holy Eucharist, the visits and encouragement of the chaplain. Now, at one stroke, she was deprived of all this, and the void it created plunged her soul into agony.

To add to her spiritual sufferings were the blows that the war was dealing to her natural affections. She deeply loved her native land and her fellow countrymen, and her father's cruelty had failed to lessen her affection for him. But from the servant she learned that the enemy had advanced far into the land, that many soldiers had been killed, and that her father's life was constantly in great jeopardy.

The medieval biographer observes that "the Evil One was desperately endeavoring to break the girl's spirit by this accumulation of trials." But although Margaret was severely tried by the ordeal, her faith and courage enabled her to emerge victorious. But she would need even greater and greater courage for the tragedy that was approaching her.

Chapter VI

THE GERMAN PILGRIMS

Montefeltro's plan for a swift advance was jeopardized when some of his soldiers set fire to the farmhouses near the border. The many columns of smoke warned the natives of the presence of the invaders, and everywhere men rushed to arms. Soon Parisio had his men in strategic positions to slow down the enemy advance. The Trabarians fought with such courage that the enemy advance began to fall behind in its time schedule. To his dismay, Montefeltro found that a week's fighting had gained him—not three-fourths of the country—but only one-third of it.

At this juncture, Malatesta of Rimini, the archenemy of Montefeltro, learning of the invasion of Trabaria, attacked Urbino in the north. Montefeltro was forced to rush his army north to repel the invaders of his own country. However, he left behind a force large enough to hold the territory he had conquered.

In the brief lull that followed, hundreds of men from nearby states volunteered to fight under Parisio. He soon found he had an army strong enough to take the offensive. Months of fighting ensued, and by the end of summer, the Urbinians were driven out of the land. The approach of winter put an end to hostilities, but in the spring the war was resumed.

Parisio crossed the border of Urbino and began a series of raids, slaying the natives and burning the farmhouses and barns. Montefeltro now had to fight on two fronts, with Malatesta on the north and Parisio on the south. Montefeltro dared not weaken his northern army to send any sizable force against Parisio, so the latter continued to devastate southern Urbino. Finally, Montefeltro made a treaty of peace with Parisio and pledged not to attack Trabaria in the future.

By now, time had disclosed two of the three events that would deeply affect Margaret; it was now about to present the third event—in itself an unimportant episode. Like most

27

medieval towns, Mercatello had a great square or *piazza*. As in most cities, it was bounded by a cathedral, the town hall and the residences or *palazzi* of the wealthier citizens. It was the center of town life, and the people, dressed in gaily colored robes, would gather there daily, the men to discuss politics, the women to buy provisions and exchange gossip.

During the month of August, 1307, the *piazza* had been rife with reports that Montefeltro was offering peace terms to Trabaria—the giant was asking the pigmy to make peace!

But this wonderful news would soon be rivalled by the news five German pilgrims would bring to Mercatello. It was near noon when the guards at the south gate saw a group of five men approaching the town. Their gray robes with gray mantles, their round felt hats, the staves they carried, and the scrip or small leather bag slung over the shoulder of each man proclaimed they were pilgrims. Such men were always welcome, since they brought news from distant cities. The people in the *piazza* began to draw near the city gate, when someone noticed the loden emblems sewn to the hats of the pilgrims. Excitedly he shouted:

"The cross keys and the vernacle! The pilgrims are from Rome!"

At this, everybody rushed toward the pilgrims, who were now close, and began to deluge them with questions about the Pope, Clement V. As everybody was shouting his questions at the same time, the uproar prevented the replies of the pilgrims from being heard. Then a stentorian voice was heard from the fringe of the crowd. "Silence! Silence! Everybody, silence!"

The speaker was a tall, burly man, strikingly dressed. He wore a long gown of yellow silk over which was a scarlet cloak, while a red cape with the hood thrown back covered his shoulders. As all three garments were trimmed in ermine, it was evident that their owner was a man of wealth. Indeed, he was none other than Messer Rainaldo, magistrate of Mercatello. When he had obtained silence, he said to the pilgrims:

"While you were at the Eternal City, did you learn when the Pope will leave France and return to Rome?"

The chief pilgrim sadly replied:

"When we left Rome ten days ago, there was an official statement to the effect that Clement V intends to reside permanently at Avignon."

A stunned silence followed this information. Men gazed at one another in utter disbelief, wondering if they had heard right. A Pope live elsewhere than at Rome? The very thought was preposterous! The silence was broken by a Franciscan friar shouting as he threw up his arms: "There must be a curse on all Italy! Wars are breaking out everywhere from Sicily to the Alps—there is bloodshed and crime on all sides! And now even the Pope has abandoned us! God is angry with us because of our sins!"

"A son of St. Francis should not say that," answered the pilgrim mildly. "In view of what one Franciscan is doing near here, it is evident God is not angry with everybody in Italy!"

"What do you mean?" asked the friar, obviously surprised.

"Have you not heard of Fra Giacomo of Castello? No? He was a lay member of your Order—a tertiary. I say 'was' because he recently died and many people claim miracles have been performed at his tomb."

"Miracles at Castello?" protested one tradesman who believed anything might happen in far-off places, but not close at hand.

"What is so strange about that?" indignantly demanded Messer Rainaldo. "Didn't the *Poverello* himself work miracles at Castello?"

"Yes!" jubilantly shouted the friar. "And now we have another Franciscan wonder-worker nearby!"

The servant who brought Margaret her meals told her that the war was over. Trabaria was safe, and in a short time her father would be returning. The news filled the girl with a happiness she had rarely known. What more could one desire? Bloodshed was ended, her country free again, her father unharmed! She fell to her knees to thank God for that triple blessing. Had she been able to look into the future, her joy would have quickly come to an end. For tragedy, a grim tragedy, was patiently waiting for her. And it would not have to wait long.

Chapter VII

THE SHRINE AT CASTELLO

In September, the victorious Parisio returned home. He disbanded his army and then made a full report of the war to the *podesta* and the State Council. When these lengthy meetings were over, the Captain rejoined his wife, who was still at Mercatello. In the days that followed, Emilia undertook to bring her husband up to date on local happenings. In doing so, she came in due time to the report of the pilgrims that miraculous cures were taking place at Castello. Parisio burst out laughing.

"Don't tell me, my dear wife, that you believe in miracles!"

"Well, after all," she replied defensively, "everybody admits St. Francis possessed a remarkable healing power."

"True, while he was alive. Some few men seem to have such a power. But since this Giacomo is dead, it would mean that miracles are taking place. Miracles presuppose that God is deeply interested in us—which, you know as well as I do, is sheer nonsense."

Nonsense or not, fresh reports continued to reach Mercatello with almost every traveller. Some of these men were well educated; occasionally there was a professor, or a lawyer, or even a physician. When men of their standing insisted that cures were being effected at the tomb of Fra Giacomo, Parisio began to waver a little in his incredulity. His wife was quick to take advantage of his change of attitude.

"Parisio, why don't we take Margaret to Citta di Castello? Who knows? Perhaps she will be cured both of her blindness and her deformities! At least there's a possibility."

"It is a rough, hard journey over the mountains," replied her husband hesitantly.

"I can stand it. If we leave early in the morning, let us say about the hour of Prime, we should reach there certainly by sunset."

Emilia waited anxiously for his reply. She had never seen

Citta di Castello, and for that reason was eager to go there. And of course, one never could tell, there was a possibility of Margaret's being cured. But Parisio still hesitated.

"Frankly, my dear, I don't know what to do with the creature. We cannot leave her here; it is too dangerous. On the other hand, I do not want to risk taking her back to Metola, because this so-called peace is not going to last very long."

"That is all the more reason why we should seize the chance of going now. In any case, we have nothing to lose!"

Parisio, who had been pacing up and down the room, stopped short and cast a startled glance at his wife. Then he repeated, almost to himself:

"We have nothing to lose!"

After a few moments' reflection he added briskly:

"Very well, then, we'll go. Today is the 20th of September; can you be ready by the 24th? Good! We will depart at early dawn, before the citizens are astir."

Now that she had gained her end, Lady Emilia became somewhat uneasy.

"Of course, Parisio, we have no assurance that Margaret will be cured. But I have heard the Franciscan friar, who preaches in the *piazza*, declare that all one needs is faith. Margaret certainly has plenty of that!"

"We'll cross that bridge when we come to it, my dear," replied her husband, who was now in sudden good humor. "Remember: Thursday morning at early dawn. Emilia, I think, in fact I know, that this pilgrimage will definitely solve our problem."

The Captain left the room.

Lady Emilia shivered as if a sudden chill had pervaded the apartment. She did not understand, nor dared she ask, the meaning of his remark, and her recollection of his many acts of ruthlessness did nothing to reassure her.

The night before the pilgrimage, Lady Emilia did not sleep too well. The thought of the exciting journey over the Apennine Mountains to a city she had never seen, and the probability of being forever freed—either by a miracle or by some other means—of the nightmare of a deformed daughter, wrought her feelings to such a pitch that for a long time sleep eluded her. Notwithstanding, at first cockcrow she awoke and hastened to arouse her husband and Margaret.

It did not take them long to get ready, as every possible preparation had been made the day before. Their mounted escort, consisting of a dozen men-at-arms whom Parisio had carefully chosen, was already outside the main entrance, their horses neighing and pawing the ground, impatient to get started. At the sight of the soldiers, Lady Emilia was reassured; she would have nothing to fear from the bandits who lurked in the lonelier stretches of the forest, waiting to attack unprotected travellers.

The church bell had barely begun to sound the hour of Prime when Parisio gave the order and all mounted their horses. In the dim uncertain light of early morning, as the party approached the southern gate of the city, a challenge rang out. Instantly the travellers halted. Then Parisio advanced at a slow pace, while he shook back his fur-trimmed hood so that the guards might see his face. The officer of the guard stepped forward to question him; as he did so, he recognized his commander and saluted him.

"Your Excellency! The Captain of the People!"

"Open the gate," ordered Parisio curtly, "and lower the drawbridge. Quick! It's urgent."

The soldiers ran to comply with his orders, and they watched with curiosity as the party, everyone completely muffled in their cloaks as protection against the cold morning air, silently filed through the gate. The soldiers noticed the two women and assumed—for they could not see their faces—that they were Lady Emilia and her serving maid, returning to the castle of Metola. But contrary to the expectation of the guard, the travellers turned in the opposite direction and soon were swallowed up in the morning fog.

Until the rising sun had dispelled the fog, progress was slow because of the wretchedness of the road. The present-day tourist, journeying from Mercatello to Citta di Castello, travels over a wide, splendid highway that crosses the Apennine ranges in long, easy grades. But the only road available to Parisio was a miserable unpaved one, barely wide enough

"Tomorrow morning, Margaret," said Parisio, "your mother and I will take you to the Franciscan church. We can go to Confession and receive Holy Communion before we pray for your cure."

Lady Emilia stared in astonishment at her husband. Confession? Communion? Noticing her stunned look, Parisio gave her a reassuring gesture; with relief, Emilia realized the talk about the Sacraments had been solely for their daughter's benefit.

"I want you, my dear child," continued Parisio, "to pray tonight and tomorrow morning with your whole heart and soul for a complete cure. You will obey me in this matter, won't you, Margaret?"

"Oh, yes, Father! With all my heart!"

It was the first time her father had ever called her his "dear child!" Never had her parents spoken so kindly to her, and—what was more important to her—never had she heard them mention Confession and Communion until this day. She was so happy that tears of joy began to trickle down her cheeks. How fortunate she was to have such wonderful parents!

She would soon learn just how fortunate she was and how wonderful her parents could be.

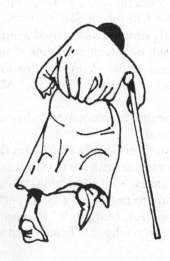

for a cart. There were no bridges across the occasional mour
tain streams, but fortunately, during autumn the water wa
low. As the road took a fairly direct line to Citta di Castello
many of the grades were steep and dangerous. It was
journey that put to severe test both the endurance and th
surefootedness of the horses.

When the Captain and his party at long last had climbed t
the top of the last mountain ridge, they saw a panorama tha
made them forget, at least for the time being, the discomfor
of the journey. Far below them stretched a long, wide, pic
turesque valley through which flowed the Tiber. Nestling i
the plain on the east bank of the river lay the historic town c
Citta di Castello, the *Tifernum Tiberinum* of the ancier
Romans. The high, strong walls completely encircling th
city, the towers rising at frequent intervals along these wall
the palaces and churches with their lofty towers and spire
all united to form an impressive picture. Unlike Perugia c
Assisi, the town was on level ground and the travellers coul
see the entire city spread out before them.

Parisio's first care upon entering the city was to procure
accommodations at the best inn, for Lady Emilia declare
herself exhausted by the long arduous journey. So, while th
womenfolk rested, the Captain set forth to gather what infc
mation he might concerning the Franciscan shrine. He beg
his inquiries at the Church of San Francesco, and before
finished his investigation he had visited a considerable par
the town. As a result he became convinced that genuine cu
were being effected at the shrine of Fra Giacomo. For
first time he began to entertain hope that Margaret migh
cured.

Returning to the inn, he recounted to his wife and dau
what he had learned.

"I have talked to three people who claim they were cu
checked their statements with their relatives and with r
bors, and in two cases, with their physicians. I am no
vinced that genuine miracles have been performed."

"Isn't that wonderful, Margaret!" exclaimed Lady I
"There is every reason why this Franciscan saint shou
you, too!"

Chapter VIII

MARGARET IS GIVEN HER FREEDOM

The next morning the little group went to church at the hour of Terce. Although the blind girl never suspected it, she was the only one who went to Confession and received Holy Communion. When the Mass was ended, her parents stationed her as close to the tomb of Fra Giacomo as they could get her, and again whispered their command for her to pray with all her might. Then they withdrew some distance from the shrine because of the crowd. Their daughter, they noticed, quickly became absorbed in prayer, utterly unmindful of the noise and confusion about her. After watching her for some time, they grew bored and went for a stroll about the town.

"We must be reasonable, Emilia," said Parisio. "It may take God some time to perform the miracle we want! But I now feel certain we shall get it!"

"What has made you so confident?"

"Something I thought of while I was watching the rabble at the shrine. You and I, Emilia, come from the two best families of our Republic. It isn't every day that people of the highest nobility visit this shrine! If God listens to persons of mean extraction, it is certain that He will listen to us!"

"That is true!" cried Emilia. "I hadn't thought of that!"

When the couple had finished their leisurely sight-seeing, they returned to the church in high hopes. Coming from the bright, sunlit street into the dark building, they were unable at first to distinguish Margaret among the many people surrounding the shrine. Then they saw her. She was still rapt in profound prayer, unconscious of the bustle and confusion about her. When Parisio and Emilia approached close to the girl they saw something else. No miracle had taken place!

The nobleman and his wife stood fixed on the spot. At last the Captain plucked the sleeve of Emilia and motioned her to follow him. When they reached the street, they stood looking

at each other, utterly disgusted with God's failure to respect their rank.

Emilia was on the verge of tears.

"What are we going to do with her, Parisio?" she wailed. "We cannot take her back to Mercatello!"

"No, that is out of the question. Since God is not going to help us, we shall solve the problem in our own way. Come!"

Without so much as a glance at the church where their daughter was, they returned to the inn. Their escort was notified to get ready to leave. Parisio settled his bill and the party rode out of the city by the northeast gate, the Porta Sant'Egidio.

The blind cultivate their sense of hearing to such a degree that when people approach them, they can usually recognize their different friends merely by listening to their footsteps. During the remaining years of Margaret's life she would hear the footsteps of thousands of people. But no matter how long or how attentively she would listen, never again would she hear the footsteps of the two persons she knew so well. For the noble lord and lady of Metola had abandoned their daughter.

Already they were several miles away, unmercifully spurring their horses and pushing on as rapidly as the terrain would allow. They were anxious to reach Mercatello before nightfall, because travelling over that mountain road in the dark was perilous. Perhaps, too, the Captain and his wife were trying to flee their consciences. But no matter how hard they rode, to the day of their death Parisio and Emilia would never be able to escape the pursuing image of a hapless blind girl, alone in a strange city, trustfully waiting for the return of the father and mother she loved more than life itself.

When Margaret's parents had stationed her near the shrine of Fra Giacomo they had told their daughter that they would wait for her in another part of the church, because here they would be in the way of other pilgrims. It was a valid excuse for their not staying with her: already the number of ailing and crippled persons assembled at the shrine was large and was steadily increasing.

In obedience to her parents' commands, Margaret had at

once addressed herself to God, begging Him to cure her of her various deformities. But she laid down one condition for her cure:

"Grant me these favors, I implore Thee, dearest God, but only provided my cure is in accordance with Thy will. If Thou dost desire me to bear these burdens until death, I am content to do so. I ask only that Thy will be done."

During the years of her incarceration Margaret had developed an extraordinary love for prayer. Hence, while the other petitioners at the shrine gradually grew tired and left the church, Margaret persevered. And throughout her lengthy prayers there continued to run one refrain: "I ask this favor only if it is in accordance with Thy will."

As the day wore on, Margaret heard the church bells announce at high noon the hour for Sext, and again at mid-afternoon the hour of None. The girl was beginning to feel faint, as she had had nothing to eat or drink since supper the night before. Then the bells of the whole city broke into a tumultuous clamor as they proclaimed Vespers, thus marking the end of the day. And still her parents did not approach her.

With increasing insistence the thought presented itself that there was something very strange in the conduct of her parents, but the loyal girl rejected the thought every time with the reflection that they undoubtedly had good reasons for their delay. Her 14 years in prison had taught her how to wait; when her parents were ready, they would call her. So, tranquilly, she resumed her meditations.

At length a voice did arouse her, but it was not the voice of her father or mother. It was the voice of the Franciscan lay brother who was sexton of the church.

"It is time to close the church. Everybody leave, please! Time to close the church!"

At these words dismay filled the heart of the blind girl as she realized their full import. Her parents were not in the church! She could readily understand why they might have grown tired of waiting, or perhaps had some affairs to attend to in the city; in either case, they left without speaking to her lest they disturb her devotions. But why had they not sent one of the soldiers for her? Her thoughts were in a turmoil.

Meanwhile the sexton continued to make his rounds of the church, loudly jingling his bunch of keys and chanting his warning, as if it were the response to a litany. Then abruptly the response was changed:

"Little girl! What are you doing here at this late hour? You should have been home long ago! Run!"

The nearness of the voice led Margaret to believe that the words were meant for her. Getting to her feet with difficulty, because of her weariness and stiffness, she held out her hand and said:

"Brother, I am blind. Please guide me to the door."

Her voice arrested the attention of the friar, and holding his lantern up to her face, he demanded:

"How old are you?"

"I am 20 years old." Then, recalling that he had called her a little girl, she added, smiling, "You see, Brother, I am a midget; I suppose my size misled you."

Embarrassed over his mistake, the friar hastily took her arm and began to lead her to the entrance, wondering all the while whether she was really blind. He did not mind the many beggars who clustered at the church door every day, but his wrath was enkindled by the knaves who pretended to be cripples—rogues so adept at simulating physical deformities that they seemed more pitiable than did the genuine cripples. This girl did not seem to be an imposter; still, you could never be certain. He asked skeptically:

"If you are blind, and a stranger here, how did you find your way to the shrine in the first place?"

"My parents brought me here."

"Your parents?" he echoed. "And where are they now, pray?"

"I do not know."

The friar shook his head, and as he reached the door, paused irresolutely. There was something about this blind cripple that set her apart from other people. Was it her evident refinement? Or was it something intangible he could not quite place? To his surprise, he found himself saying:

"I am sorry I must leave you on the church steps. But you understand, don't you, that I must close and lock the church doors? Godless thieves loiter in this *piazza* and they would not hesitate to steal from the church! Only last week a pair of silver candlesticks were stolen from the Madonna chapel by some—." The outraged friar stammered in his effort to describe adequately anyone so depraved as to rob the Madonna chapel!

"I understand, Brother," Margaret replied gently. "Do not worry about me. My parents will surely be along any moment now."

As the friar locked the doors, he could hardly help reflecting on how great was the contrast between her wretched appearance and her sweet, gentle voice. But in a short time, occupied in the press of his duties, he had forgotten her existence.

For some time Margaret stood in the doorway waiting. Then, realizing how tired she was, she sat on the stone step.

The increasing cold told her that the night was advancing. Suppose her parents did not return? Where could she spend the night? She could not ask someone to lead her to the inn, because she did not know its name. She recalled now that she had asked her parents what the inn's name was but they had not answered her question. Nor could she go to any other inn, as she had no money. To attempt to go from door to door, hoping some kindhearted person would give her refuge for the night, would mean venturing into strange, unfamiliar streets—a hazardous thing for a blind person to attempt.

The plight in which the girl found herself can be appreciated only by the blind, and to a lesser degree by persons who understand something of the world of the blind. Contrary to a widespread belief, nature does not compensate the blind man for his privation by endowing him with a "sixth sense." Because the blind do not have sight, they must make greater use of their other senses; and they naturally make better use of them than does a seeing person who relies on them only to a limited degree. Thus the average blind person can move unhesitatingly about a room or building with which he is familiar, and he can make his way through the city streets—provided he has been guided over them often enough to memorize their characteristics. But in a new, strange locality, the blind person who becomes separated from his guide is indeed lost.

Margaret, therefore, would have been extremely imprudent had she ventured to explore, unassisted, the streets of the town, for she would have met dangers rarely found in a modern city. Citta di Castello, like most medieval towns, had only a few paved streets; the rest were of dirt and they became slippery lanes of mud whenever it rained. Most thoroughfares were narrow and without sidewalks. The rubbish and garbage which were thrown into the streets rendered them dangerous not only to the blind but even to pedestrians who had their sight. But this was not all: a large number of animals—dogs, pigs, goats and even cows—roamed the streets and were apt to lie down anywhere they pleased. Nightfall brought an added danger: the city streets were not lighted and a belated wayfarer ran the risk of falling into the hands of criminals who prowled about the dark streets.

But serious as these dangers were, they did not constitute the principal reason for Margaret's remaining where she was. When her parents returned, they would be alarmed at not finding her at the church, and they would not know where to look for her. Doubtless they would begin a frantic search and thus pass the night consumed with anxiety for her safety. Rather than expose her parents to such distress, she preferred to remain at the church door, even though she was cold, hungry, and frightened.

The knowledge that her parents did not love her did indeed engender the thought that they had deserted her, but Margaret instantly rejected the thought. No, something terrible must have happened. Perhaps they had been caught in one of those frequent and bloody street brawls between the Guelphs and Ghibellines, and had been seriously injured. Then, too, since Massa Trabaria was occasionally at war with Citta di Castello, perhaps some local nobleman had recognized Parisio and seized him and his wife to settle old grudges. Margaret shuddered at the thought. She knew it was a common practice for noblemen to take the law into their own hands and wreak fearful vengeance on their enemies.

"I may as well face it," thought the girl. "I may never again meet my dear father and mother. From now on I may have to face the future alone."

It was a situation for which she was totally unprepared. From childhood she had always been provided with the essentials she needed: food, clothing, shelter, security. During the long 14 years she had spent in prison she had never experienced the need, or been given the opportunity, of developing her senses to their highest degree in compensation for her blindness. Now, without warning, she was confronted with the probability of having to rely wholly on her own efforts for everything she needed—for she was in a strange town with neither relatives nor friends. She realized that, as she had no money, she would have to beg for a living.

But that would mean that she would have to sleep on the streets and have as her associates men and women who were the dregs of the city: professional beggars, knaves, thieves, and even worse. It was a future that might well have filled a young and refined woman with horror and despair.

The various sounds that now began to reach Margaret's ears announced that the night was finally ending and that the sleeping city was coming to life. For the blind girl, it was a dawn of dreadful apprehension, because before sunset she would surely know the answer to the fears which had beset her during the long night. Courageous as she was, she could not avoid being fearful of what that answer might be.

Chapter IX

THE HOMELESS BEGGAR

It was September 26, the Feast of St. Amantius, one of the patrons of Citta di Castello. Of course, he was not so great as St. Floridus, the principal patron, but still many clients would honor him by going to church. Remembering this fact, two beggars, Roberto and Elena, hurried early to the Franciscan church, hoping to be the first beggars there so that they might have a monopoly of the alms.

The streets were still dark, although the first hint of dawn was in the sky. Despite the penetrating cold, the two beggars were in high spirits until they rounded the corner and entered the small *piazza* in front of San Francesco. There they stopped short, for despite the early hour, someone was at the church door ahead of them. Whoever it was, was trying to keep warm by walking up and down in the doorway.

Elena peered in the dim, uncertain light.

"It is a woman—a cripple," she said. "I don't recognize her; she must be a stranger."

The man and woman looked at each other; they knew all the regular members of this church and there was no crippled woman among them. This creature must be a beggar, come to steal the bread out of their mouths!

"We'll soon send her back to where she came from!" exclaimed the indignant Roberto. "The impudence of her— trespassing on our territory! Come, Elena!"

Angrily the two advanced toward the intruder. But their hostility quickly ended when they learned that the crippled blind girl was not a beggar. They listened in surprise to the strange story of her parents' disappearance. Meanwhile, in the growing light, Elena had been closely looking at the dress and cloak of the blind girl. Pulling Roberto a little to one side, she whispered, "The clothes she is wearing are expensive; her parents must be rich. Maybe we can earn a big reward by returning her to them."

43

Aroused by this hope, they now took the keenest interest in Margaret, and plied her with questions; but there was little she could tell them beyond the fact that she came from Mercatello and had passed the night at the inn near the city gate.

"*Per Bacco!*" exclaimed Roberto disconsolately. "Much help that is, with a score of inns in the town!"

"Wait a moment!" cried Elena. "You said that after you entered the city gate it did not take long to reach the inn. When you came to church yesterday, did you walk or ride?"

"We walked."

"Did it seem a great distance to you?"

"No, it did not."

"We have it, Roberto!" cried Elena in triumph. "They are staying at the Blue Boar!"

Slow-witted Roberto looked bewildered.

"Look, Roberto. Coming from Mercatello, they must have entered the city by the Porta Sant'Egidio—which is close by. They came to visit the shrine, so they would naturally seek suitable lodgings not far away. Now there are only two places in this part of town where wealthy people would put up: the Crouching Lion, and the Blue Boar. The Lion is a good distance from here; if her parents are staying there, they would have come to the church on horseback, since the young lady limps badly. The Blue Boar, on the other hand, is only a short distance away. I tell you, Roberto, it must have been the Blue Boar."

Elena's deductions proved correct. The innkeeper recognized Margaret, but he said:

"The people you came with left yesterday. As they rode in the direction of the Porta Sant'Egidio, I assumed that they were leaving town."

"Oh, that is not possible!" cried Margaret. "There must be some other explanation."

"It will be a simple matter to find out if they left," declared Roberto. "The Porta Sant'Egidio is not far from here. We will ask the guards."

It was a good suggestion. In the days when enemies used every form of trickery to capture a city, without even a previous declaration of war, military security demanded that a strict watch be kept on all strangers. If, therefore, Parisio and Emilia were still in the city, the guards would have a record of it.

Trembling, Margaret put her question to the officer of the guard. His answer was brief and stupefying.

"They left here yesterday, shortly before high noon, and took the road to Mercatello. From the way they spurred their horses, you would have thought the devil himself was after them!"

At this reply Margaret's little world came crashing down about her. From childhood she had known that her parents did not love her, but now, for the first time, she learned that they actually hated her and were determined to be forever rid of her. Noticing how stunned the girl was, the beggar Elena, moved by pity, placed her arm around her and exclaimed:

"You poor forlorn child! How could they be so cruel to you!"

"Oh! Oh!" muttered Roberto disconsolately. "There goes softhearted Elena again! Every time that woman meets a hungry dog or a famished brat she has to feed it, instead of looking out for herself! Now she'll take care of this cripple till the creature can take care of herself."

For a while Margaret neither saw nor heard those around her; she was completely numbed by the news which even yet she could scarcely believe. As she began to recover somewhat from the shock, she realized that she was being offered another opportunity to resemble her Savior, who also had been abandoned by His friends. Although her soul was tried to its very depths by the blow, Margaret heroically forced her rebellious will to accept the cross. In her agony, she besought God that she might more perfectly devote herself to Him, her heavenly Father, now that she no longer had an earthly father.

Meanwhile, the sympathetic group of people who had gathered around her were expressing in no uncertain terms their opinions of Margaret's parents. As the girl regained control of herself, she became aware for the first time of the vituperation being heaped upon her father and mother. At once she spoke in their defense. Had they not taken care of her for 20 years? Why should they be burdened with her all their life? It was high time for her to start taking care of herself, and this is precisely what she intended to do!

"Do you have any friends here in Citta di Castello?" asked the practical Elena. "No? Have you any money? No? Then in that case, the sooner you start learning how to beg the better. Come, I'll show you a good place to station yourself. If things get too bad for you, the other beggars will try to help you; that's our rule."

So her new companions, the outcasts of the city, taught Margaret the streets of the town, leading her over them again and again until she had memorized them well enough to make her way alone. It was the human derelicts who showed the location of the fountains where she might wash and slake her thirst, and the most sheltered doorways where she might sleep at night without being driven away by the suspicious night patrol.

That year the winter was unusually severe. Even before the first of November, the surrounding mountains were covered with snow; then, on the Feast of St. Martin, while the shivering citizens gathered close to their hearths, Citta di Castello was visited by a raging snowstorm. Late in the afternoon Elena searched in the usual haunts of Margaret and finally found the blind girl covered with snow and huddled in a doorway.

"Little Margaret, you cannot sleep here tonight; you'll freeze to death. I asked Pietro, the carpenter, if we could sleep in his stable tonight and he said 'Yes.'"

"Sleep in a stable!" exclaimed Margaret in tones of wonder.

"Yes," returned Elena in surprise. "The place is dirty and the smell is terrible, it is true, but after all, we beggars can hardly be choosers."

"Oh, Elena, I didn't mean that. I was thinking that Our Lord was born in a stable, and God is going to allow us to pass the night in one! It will be just like Bethlehem! How good God is to us, Elena!"

Elena stared at her friend, open-mouthed.

"God? What has God to do with it? If you ask me, it is the

carpenter who is being good to us."

"Dear Elena, it was God who put the idea in your mind, and it was God who moved the carpenter to give you permission. God will surely bless both of you for your kindness."

"God doesn't know I exist," said Elena bitterly, "and if He saw me coming, He would take to His heels. And don't be talking about my goodness; I am just a rotten little tramp."

Margaret pressed the arm of her companion affectionately.

"Dearest Elena, I love you as if you were my own sister. And, what is more important, God loves you no matter what you may have done. Dearest friend, if you would only try to love God who hungers even for the love of 'tramps,' you would find peace and happiness."

Not wishing to hurt her friend's feelings, Elena made no reply, and in silence the two made their way to the stable.

No native of Citta di Castello would have dreamed of pointing out to a visitor Pietro's dilapidated stable as one of the historically important places in the town; yet on that cold winter night history was made in the lowly shelter—at least for one human being—just as centuries ago history was made for the whole human race in another stable.

For a long time the two outcasts lay in the straw, each one feigning sleep for fear of disturbing the other. Margaret was reflecting on the scene at Bethlehem when Christ was born. So vivid was her meditation that she felt as though the Savior were really present, with His Mother and St. Joseph. It was then she heard a whisper, so faint that even her keen hearing barely caught it:

"God, I didn't know You cared for me; I'm sorry for all the bad things I've done. And God, please don't let any more troubles come to little Margaret; she isn't like me."

Elena then fell asleep, but Margaret was recalling what the Dominican friar, Fra Luigi, had said the previous Sunday: "When we stop making ourselves the center of all our cares, and start thinking how we can genuinely help our fellowman, then we are beginning to draw near to God." The "little tramp" had started back on the right road. Now Margaret was certain that the reason why her meditation on Bethlehem had been so realistic was because the Savior had just paid a second visit to a stable.

"I don't see, Maria, how you can stand talking for half the day to that horrible-looking cripple."

"I wasn't talking to her very long, and she isn't horrible-looking," protested Maria, the wife of Carlo the Notary. "I find her interesting. Do you know, Antonina, she is truly an amazing girl! Truly amazing!"

"What is amazing about her? She is just another beggar. If you ask me, there are already too many of them in town."

Antonina was not usually cross, but although her husband was a well-to-do draper, she was greatly upset because the price of meat had gone up again, this time three *denari* a pound.

"Just think, Antonina! She has nothing—not even a room to sleep in at night—and she is as happy as the day is long!"

"I don't believe it! Why, what has she to be happy about?"

"She is happy, she told me, because God loves us so much."

"Maria!" cried Antonina heatedly. "Use a little common sense! No one could suffer like that wretched cripple and be happy about it. *Mamma mia!* Even a saint would find it almost impossible."

Her companion stopped short and stared wide-eyed at her friend.

"What's the matter, Maria? Why are you staring at me like that?"

"Excuse me, dear," said Maria breathlessly. "You don't mind going home alone, do you? I must return to Margaret. I think you have hit the nail right on the head!"

With that she was gone.

Antonina stood gazing at Maria flying down the street. Then, shaking her head in bewilderment at the strange conduct of her companion, she resumed her homeward journey.

"What in the world did she mean when she said I hit the nail on the head?"

Chapter X

MARGARET ENTERS THE CONVENT

Maria and Antonina were not the only ones in Citta di Castello who were arguing about the blind cripple. In ever widening circles the controversy spread. Was Margaret really sincere, or was she simply an extremely clever girl who realized that an attitude of cheerfulness, forgiveness and patience would win for her greater assistance than would despondency and bitterness? As a result of these arguments, she was closely watched—with admiration by her growing numbers of friends, with suspicion by the incredulous.

As month after month went by and Margaret successfully stood the test of public disbelief, the attitude of the citizens gradually changed to one of warmest admiration. While the wealthy people as yet held themselves aloof from the beggar, the poor who had "discovered" Margaret decided that she should not be obliged to live any longer as a miserable vagabond. They solved the problem by inviting her into their homes. But because the purses of the poor were not as big as their hearts, no one family could afford to take permanent care of her. Each family simply did what it could. Each gave Margaret a home as long as possible; when the economic strain became too great for that household's meager income, another family would come to the rescue and invite the girl to share their humble hospitality. Thus, for several years, she passed from house to house, from family to family.

It was a surprising situation—a homeless beggar being practically adopted by the poor of a city; we know of no similar instance in the annals of history. Margaret had indeed lost her family home, but she had acquired a large number of homes in exchange. If the dwellings of the poor were not so spacious or so well furnished as her father's castle, at least they were not prisons. And it was in the homes of the poor that the blind girl experienced for the first time what her heart had hungered for during her life, and what her own parents had denied her: a warm welcome, sincere affection and unselfish love.

Any lingering doubts the more incredulous citizens might have entertained concerning the genuineness of Margaret's virtues were dispelled by her continued dwelling with the poor. Indeed, it was an acid test for a person of refinement to live, over an extended period of time, in such homes. They were small and overcrowded, and all day long they resounded with the uproar of many children. Of privacy there was none. Even the sleeping room was occupied by as many as eight or ten persons; all slept on the floor.

But this was not all. The floors were made of a mixture of sand and rushes, trampled to hardness. As dogs, cats, hens and pigs roamed quite freely through the house, and the flooring was rarely—if ever—changed, the odor must have been very unpleasant to a girl who had been reared on the clean wind-swept mountains. The daily fire, used for cooking or for heating, was built on a stone slab or in a dirt-filled box in the middle of the room. As there was no chimney or vent of any kind, the house was generally filled with smoke. Perhaps this was welcomed as a partial relief against flies and other vermin.

But the physical discomforts were far easier for Margaret to accept than were the social and moral conditions she found in many homes. Some families were constantly quarrelling; in others, suspicion, misunderstandings, and mutual hatred rendered home life unbearable. In many homes she found religious indifference, and, in some, hostility to the Church. But no matter how unpleasant conditions were, Margaret remained unruffled. Even in the most difficult situations, her kindness, patience, and cheerfulness seemed truly inexhaustible.

Then a strange thing became apparent. It was not noticed until a long time had passed. Every home that offered hospitality to Margaret gradually underwent a marked change. Mario the baker and his wife had been forever quarrelling; now they were more tolerant of each other's faults. Pietro the carpenter and his wife had been completely discouraged by their persistent misfortunes; they were now cheerful and optimistic. Neighbors who had been hostile to one another were now friendly, and irreligious families were at last devoting serious thought to the question of their eternal salvation.

Nor were the changes that appeared to follow Margaret's sojourn at any house solely in the moral order. Destitute families invariably found that—contrary to reason—their material fortunes had improved instead of becoming worse. When this phenomenon was noticed, the people attributed it to Margaret's asking God to reward those who sheltered her.

These and similar stories were widely circulated throughout the town. Among those who listened with more than ordinary interest were the cloistered nuns of St. Margaret's Monastery—an old convent situated near the southeast gate of the city—the Porta Santa Maria. The medieval biography tactfully refrains from mentioning the name of the Order to which the nuns belonged. A modern historian of Citta di Castello, the erudite Bishop Giovanni Musi, gave as his opinion that the nuns were Dominican. But recent research has proved conclusively the error of that opinion. The Monastery had been founded before the Dominicans came to Citta di Castello. It is true there were at that time in the city Dominican Mantellate (of whom we shall speak later), but these women lived at home, not in a convent. Oddly enough, the Monastery of St. Margaret did become a convent for Dominican Sisters, but only years after Margaret's death.

Our medieval biographer is exceptionally niggardly in giving dates, but it appears to have been a year or two after Margaret had begun to live in the homes of the poor that she became the subject of lively debate at the convent in question. Influential benefactors represented to the nuns the plight of the blind cripple; they suggested that a girl of her refinement and character should not be tossed around from house to house, and that the proper place for her was in the monastery. The suggestions finally became so pointed that the Prioress called a meeting of her Council to discuss the matter.

It was not an easy matter to decide. Both Church law and the practice of the Order required certain qualifications in the candidate: irreproachable character, legitimate birth, and freedom from serious physical handicaps. The first condition offered no difficulty; the second and third did.

It was feared that Margaret would be a helpless burden on the community; but a greater difficulty was the question of her birth. Was she a legitimate child or not? Nobody knew anything about her parents, and it was well-known that the blind girl always parried questions concerning her parents, the place where she was born, and in fact, any but the most insignificant details of her life before coming to Citta di Castello. Her obvious care to shield her parents aroused suspicion as to her legitimacy. After prolonged debate it was resolved to place the whole matter before the Bishop of the diocese, and make him accept the responsibility for the decision. The Bishop gathered what information was available and sent it to the rector of the cathedral of Mercatello, for it was there that Margaret had been baptized "after a delay of many months." The only clue the Bishop could give the rector was the year of her birth. He requested certificates of Margaret's baptism and of the marriage of her parents.

The rector was dismayed at the thought of searching the Baptismal Records for the entry of a person whose family name was unknown. However, he finally found it. As the record of her baptism gave the names of her parents, it was easy to find the record of their marriage.

When the Bishop received the two certificates, he was stunned; the father of that deformed beggar was the now-famous general who had helped to defeat Montefeltro? It was unbelievable! This shock was followed by a second and worse shock: he had stumbled upon a carefully-guarded secret involving the honor of a proud and powerful family. There were many instances of the fearful vengeance taken by such families on all who incurred their anger. Only a half dozen years before, one of these powerful lords, angered at the Pope, had seized and imprisoned him. He treated his prisoner so brutally that the Pope died a month later. If the highest office in the Church was despised by these sacrilegious lords, what regard would they show to a mere bishop?

His Excellency lost no time notifying the nuns that he had learned Margaret was both legitimate and baptized. There was one item, however, he did not tell the nuns, or anyone else—the family name of the girl. After receiving this assurance from the Bishop, the nuns invited Margaret to join their community.

Needless to say, the blind girl accepted the invitation with joy. No longer would she be a burden on the poor who had so unselfishly supported her; she would not have to deprive them of the food they needed for themselves, nor put them to further inconvenience by occupying space in their already overcrowded homes. In addition, she could now devote herself to a life of prayer and work, and make excellent use of the convent's quiet solitude—a luxury she had not known in the houses of the poor!

The day on which she was conducted by her friends to the monastery and welcomed by the Sisters into their community was a day of unutterable happiness for Margaret. The nuns in turn were moved by her sincere friendliness, by her obvious gratitude, and by her wonder that everybody should be so kind to her.

The Sisters were surprised to see how quickly she familiarized herself with the different rooms and corridors of the convent. Like most people who have had no contact with the blind, the nuns had expected they would have to wait on the girl as if she were a helpless invalid. They were astonished to discover that not only could she take care of herself, but that she could clean rooms, help prepare meals, set the table in the refectory, wash kitchen utensils, and perform many similar tasks.

Margaret was so happy that she became rather uneasy; she had come to the convent to labor for the salvation of souls by prayer and sacrifice, and not to be filled with overwhelming happiness. She began to fear that, perhaps because of her sinfulness, she was not worthy to suffer any more. But on this point she was soon to be enlightened.

Chapter XI

MARGARET IS EXPELLED
FROM THE CONVENT

Despite her youth and inexperience, Margaret understood the nature of convent life. She knew that a girl entered the convent not because she was necessarily a saint, but because she wished to become one. The blind girl was too intelligent to share the popular illusion that the taking of the veil automatically, as it were, eradicated one's personal shortcomings. She realized that, normally, spiritual perfection could be acquired only after many years of the most arduous self-discipline. Consequently, the obvious imperfections and the weaknesses of the various Sisters in the monastery did not in the least disturb Margaret's peace of mind.

But there was one phase of her religious life which did perplex her. It was the same problem which, both before and after Margaret's time, has troubled the members of any religious Order that has noticeably lowered its primitive standards of discipline. In joining the community, Margaret bound herself to live according to the Rule of that Order. Now, the Rule has been drawn up by a saint of the loftiest ideals and of the courage necessary to be true to those ideals. During the lifetime of the saint, when zeal and enthusiasm ran high among his followers, the observance of the Rule was maintained at a correspondingly high level. But after his death, it was inevitable—human nature being what it was—that there should have set in a slow, almost imperceptible lessening of the severe requirements and the stern austerities of the primitive Rule. This gradual decline had now been going on for some centuries. The average novice, noticing the discrepancy between the Rule and the actual life of the nuns, would be reassured by the explanation:

"The Rule was written ages ago! Today, one could not live up to it in all its details. Times have changed too much!"

Unfortunately for Margaret's peace of mind, she was well above the average in intelligence, and furthermore possessed a candor that allowed no evasion where any moral principle was at stake. As a result, she could not reconcile the explanation with the facts.

Thus, the Rule insisted on the value of silence at certain periods of the day and night; yet this rule was ignored. Margaret heard the nuns talking day and night on unimportant subjects; conversations were freely held in the corridor, in the rooms, and even in the refectory during meals, despite the admonition of the Rule that silence be preserved in all three places at all times. The novice mistress explained to the blind girl that it was more important to be sociable ("Charity, you know, is the greatest virtue") than it was to preserve silence. But Margaret's difficulty was that she could not understand why it was not possible to be charitable and at the same time observe the Rule.

The Rule frowned on frequent visits to the parlor to entertain visitors. Yet all day long there was a stream of relatives and friends calling on the Sisters; as a result, many hours were lost in idle conversations. This practice was justified on the grounds that by encouraging visitors, the nuns had the opportunity of doing good by giving sound advice! Margaret thought (but she was too tactful to say it) that moral guidance should be left to those who had studied moral theology—the priests—and that the nuns would better assist by their prayers and sacrifices.

Again, the Rule forbade the nuns to accept any expensive gifts for their own personal use; but such acceptance had become the established custom of the monastery. Margaret was assured that this practice was not harmful "provided one did not become attached to the gifts." In short, the blind girl found that every relaxation of the Rule had its justification!

She gave much thought to the problem. She was aware that her companions in the convent had not introduced these changes, that all of them were of many years' standing. But did long-established custom justify abuses? To her, it seemed the height of inconsistency to dedicate one's life to the observance of a Rule which, one was assured, could not be observed in modern times! If the keeping of the Rule were really impossible, then why had not the Church revised the

Rule, adapting it to present-day conditions?

After carefully pondering on the matter for some time, during which she sought guidance in prayer as well as the advice of her confessor, Margaret made her decision. She had promised God to live according to the Rule; with His help, she would try her best to do so.

If the blind girl was shocked by the laxity and the spirit of worldliness in the cloister, the nuns in their turn were amused by the efforts of the new novice to observe the very letter of the Rule. Sister Emerentiana commented upon it:

"Her 'first fervor' is lasting quite a while, isn't it? I thought that she would get over it after four or five weeks, but she has been here for nearly ten months."

"I am afraid she is heading for trouble," replied Sister Lucia. "I like little Margaret, but she is going too far! Only this morning the wife of the podesta was here and she offered Margaret a beautiful, expensive silver crucifix as a personal gift. Margaret told her that she could not accept it for herself as that would be against the vow of poverty! Her Excellency was quite offended as the Prioress last year accepted a similar crucifix!"

"I do hope Margaret will get over these extreme notions," said Sister Emerentiana, who was fond of the blind girl.

"She will. Give her a little more time and she will come to her senses."

The trouble was, however, that time passed and Margaret did not "come to her senses." The matter ceased to be amusing, and the blind girl was now looked upon as peculiar, eccentric. As such, she became a disturbing factor in the convent. Her observance of the entire Rule was a quiet but effective rebuke to the other nuns, proving as it did that "first fervor" could last. The heroic and successful attempt she was making to live according to the Rule she had sworn to observe was upsetting the consciences of the Sisters. Margaret was fast becoming the most unpopular member of the community.

If she was at all conscious of the storm that was brewing, she gave no outward indication of it. Because her own character was so honest and straightforward, she took it for granted that once a girl had renounced the world by entering a convent, she would faithfully strive as long as she lived to accomplish the purpose for which she had taken the vows. The little cripple was profoundly grateful to the Sisters for having received her into their midst; she loved them with a deep, sincere love. But her love was a wholly spiritual one, and because of it she was distressed by the carelessness of the nuns, a carelessness unworthy of their vocation.

Margaret ardently longed to repay their kindness in some measure by luring them to a greater observance of their Rule. She began in a gentle, tactful way to try to influence the Sisters who were most friendly to her. Because she was fully conscious of the delicacy of her undertaking, she placed her main hope in the good example that she herself set, hoping that where words might fail, good example would prevail.

It would be pleasant to record that her diplomacy and quiet example eventually recalled the community to a realization of its high obligations, and that, owing to the entreaties and the example set by the blind girl, the spirit of charity and the strict observance of the Rule once more flourished in St. Margaret's Monastery. But historical accuracy compels us to admit that as a reformer our little blind cripple was a total failure. Her good intentions, her kind words, her unfailing example—all went for naught. Discipline remained lax.

The only effect her diplomatic and discreet campaign had was to arouse the antagonism of the whole community. The nuns resented her efforts, and they began to protest to the Mother Prioress. That unhappy superior sent for Margaret.

"Sister Margaret," said the Prioress, "I have sent for you because of the many complaints I have received regarding your conduct. I must say that I am greatly disappointed in you. On a previous occasion I explained to you that our holy Rule was written many centuries ago. Since then, conditions have considerably changed; moreover, we are more broad-minded today than people were in those bygone days. There is an old saying, 'Custom is the best interpreter of the law,' and that is the principle we follow.

"All this I have already told you, Sister, but you persist in an impossible attempt to carry out all the details of our Rule.

I know you mean well, but your singular conduct is destroying the peace of the community. I must therefore insist that you conform to the other Sisters in your everyday life."

"Reverend Mother," replied the trembling novice, "I have discussed this matter again and again with my confessor, and he assures me that what I am doing is most pleasing to God."

"That visionary!" exclaimed the Prioress disdainfully. "He is a good priest, but he is living in the clouds. If we were to follow his idealistic counsels, we would soon be starving! Sister, I do not intend to argue the matter further. I expect an immediate change in your conduct."

In deep agitation Margaret went to the chapel and knelt before the Blessed Sacrament. She realized that this was the crisis. If she carried out the command of the Prioress, she would regain the friendship of the nuns and be assured of a permanent home; if she followed her conscience, she would certainly be expelled from the convent.

Although she had not displayed her feelings, she had suffered intensely from the hostility of the Sisters. All her life her heart had been starved for love and affection, and now that she had been cast off by her parents, she also longed for security. She would have both of these if she remained in the convent; hence, the temptation for her to compromise with her conscience, lest her future be jeopardized, was a powerful one.

But desperately as she wanted peace and harmony with her Sister religious, her inherent honesty would not permit her to evade the real issue. As a mere child she had determined to serve God with her whole heart, her whole mind, her whole soul, and ever since she had faithfully striven to do so. She could not find it in her heart to begin now to give God lukewarm service. Cost what it might, she had to follow the voice of her conscience.

The whole convent knew that she had received an ultimatum from the Prioress. Consequently, when it was seen that she continued serenely and calmly to observe the Rule as if nothing had happened, the nuns were exasperated. This was regarded as formal disobedience. A veritable storm now burst upon the head of Margaret and grew to such a degree of violence that she was summarily expelled from the convent.

As the doors closed behind her, shutting her out in the street, she stood for a while as one utterly bewildered. For a second time her little world had crashed in ruins; for a second time she had been rejected by those she loved. Then the deepest despair attacked her.

"Margaret, how stupid you are! Don't you see that the more you try to serve God, the more misfortunes you encounter? What have you gained by serving Him so earnestly all your life? Fourteen years of imprisonment, and then abandonment by your parents; you have had to beg your daily food and sleep in the street. Wake up, Margaret! If you must serve God, do so in moderation, as other people do. Life will be more pleasant for you. You must compromise, Margaret, you must compromise!"

The dark, lowering clouds of doubt and cowardice came swirling in upon her soul, striving to take possession of her. Bravely, desperately, she fought against them, but the Enemy was making one supreme effort to crush her, as if he realized that never again could he hope for so propitious a moment. Accordingly, with crushing power he forced the thought upon her that it was not the nuns but God who had rejected her, that it was God who was chastising her.

"It is of no use for you to try any more, Margaret. God does not want you. Why don't you give up, and you will gain peace!"

Complete hopelessness and discouragement hovered over the girl. She struggled with all her strength to pray, but she felt that her prayers were empty, meaningless words; worse still, God seemed to be infinitely remote. But although she was apparently abandoned by God and man alike, she was not fighting her battle alone.

At the height of the conflict, just when she felt herself dangerously close to defeat, additional divine grace came pouring into her soul. She recalled how, long ago, she had offered herself to God; she had asked Him to do with her what He wished. Knowing from childhood the supreme value of suffering, she had deliberately set out on the road to Calvary. Now that God was taking her at her word, was she going to turn back? In her meditations she had constantly reflected on the physical and mental agony of Christ, especially when He was dying on the Cross, abandoned by His disciples. It was as if the dying Savior said to her from the Cross:

"Margaret, will you, too, leave Me?"

Instantly the battle was over. Stooping, the blind girl groped for her cane, which had fallen to the ground. When she stood up, her tear-stained face was once more serene. With head erect and the familiar smile on her lips, the homeless cripple went slowly tapping her way down the narrow street, ready for whatever God had in store for her. She still wanted God—at any cost, at any price.

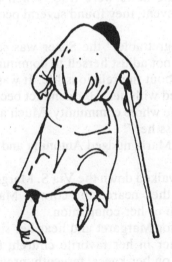

Chapter XII

MARGARET BECOMES A MANTELLATA

Antonina was prepared to go shopping as usual with her friend Maria, when Maria came rushing into the house.

"Antonina!" she cried. "Have you heard the news? There is a rumor that our little Margaret has been expelled from the monastery!"

Antonina stood for a moment speechless. Finally she gasped, "That is ridiculous! There must be some mistake!"

"Well," declared Maria resolutely, "there is only one way of finding out for certain. Let us go to the monastery!"

But on the way, their hearts sank. Person after person, knowing the two women to be close friends of Margaret, asked them if the news were true. When they entered the parlor of the convent, they found several people there talking to a nun.

"It is very regrettable," the Sister was saying, "but little Margaret could not adjust herself to community life. She had peculiar ideas about the religious life. It was in vain that the Prioress reasoned with her. Her conduct became so eccentric that she upset the whole community. Much as we regretted it, we had to dismiss her!"

Sick at heart, Maria nudged Antonina and whispered, "Let us go."

They slowly walked down the Via S. Margherita, silent and bewildered. As they neared the corner, Maria stopped and clutched the arm of her companion.

"Let us look for Margaret and hear her side of the story!"

They found her in her favorite church, the Chiesa della Carita. She was on her knees, fervently praying. At the sight of her, the loyal Maria burst into tears.

"Oh, Margaret! Margaret! What did they do to you!"

"Please don't cry, dear Maria," said the blind girl. "The Sisters were not to blame. It was all my own fault. The nuns were very kind to me and wonderfully patient."

"Kind? Patient?" Antonina choked in her rage.

"Hush, Antonina! You must not speak that way. They really were good to me. What I marvel at is that they tolerated me as long as they did! I am afraid that I am not good enough to be a nun."

Maria and Antonina looked at each other, confounded.

"Look, Margaret," sobbed Maria, "you are good enough for us. Come with us; our homes are yours."

Margaret was now to undergo a new kind of suffering—public derision and contempt. While it is true that the majority of the people at Citta di Castello had seen Margaret at one time or other, only a comparatively small number of them, probably not more than several hundred all told, had had any close association with her. Most of the people were governed by hearsay in their attitude toward the blind girl; they had heard repeated stories of the girl's extraordinary faith, courage, and cheerfulness, and, as the accounts were not contradicted, the people finally came to accept them and to hold Margaret in high esteem.

But, like all men, the citizens of Citta di Castello were more ready to believe evil than good. And so the charges against Margaret spread over the city. She is no saint, after all! The discipline of the convent was the acid test that revealed her hidden faults! She was obstinate, domineering, disobedient, a troublemaker! Many a person who secretly rejoiced at the charges because they justified his own failings, sadly shook his head and sighed:

"It is the old, old story! 'Put a beggar on horseback!'"

The children listened to the conversations of their elders, and with the cruel bluntness of children they took up the persecution. Margaret could not appear on the streets without urchins shouting at her, "Midget! Limpy! Hunchback! Here comes the 'saint!'" Margaret had thought, when she was expelled from the convent, that her chalice of suffering was filled to overflowing. Now, she realized that the cup had not been quite filled; there was room for more. Even in church she was not secure from malicious tongues; women passing near her often would make sneering remarks loud enough for her to hear.

In her agony Margaret again and again silently reaffirmed her faith and confidence in God's wisdom and love. Her divine Master had been the object of slanderous tongues; why should she be exempt? It was part of the road to Calvary. She had placed herself in the hands of God; she was not going to withdraw that trust.

After several months had gone by, the fairer-minded people of the town began to reflect on the contrast between Margaret's behavior and that of the nuns. They who by reason of their calling should have preserved a charitable silence—even if the charges were true— had advanced some serious accusations, while the girl, who had a natural right to defend herself, not only had refused to do so but even had tried to justify the Sisters!

The citizens then focused their attention more closely on the convent; from the charges levelled against Margaret, it was not difficult to deduce what the real difficulty had been. As a result, little by little the scales of public opinion changed; the convent sank low in the estimation of the people, while Margaret rose to a higher degree of esteem than ever before. Not only was Margaret's confidence in God's care of her fully justified, but there was now conferred upon her—as if in reward for her faith and courage—a gift that was to bring her solid happiness to the day of her death.

It was while Margaret was the object of almost universal contempt and ridicule that she met the Mantellate. Her favorite church was the Chiesa della Carita, in the same southeastern part of the town as the monastery, and indeed not far from it. It received its name ("the Church of Charity") from the fact that it was the official church of a society known as the "Fraternity of Charity." At this time the church was in the charge of the Dominican friars. For this reason it was also the headquarters of the Mantellate. As Margaret came there every morning to attend Mass, it was inevitable that she should become acquainted with some of the members.

Mantellate (the term is peculiar to Italy) were lay women who were members of the Order of Penance of St. Dominic— an organization that eventually developed into the present

Third Order of St. Dominic. Women who wished to live a
more religious life, but who for any reason were unable to
enter a convent, could affiliate themselves with the
Dominican Order by joining the Order of Penance. In so
doing they continued to live at home, but they bound themselves to a more religious schedule of life, and at all times,
both at home and abroad, they wore the Dominican religious
habit. This consisted of a white tunic, with a leather belt,
while over the head was worn a long, soft white veil in the
shape of an oblong scarf. There was no scapular, but the
members wore a black cloak or *mantella,* and it was this
which gave rise to the popular name of these Sisters—*Mantellate.*

Some of the Mantellate, knowing of Margaret's desire to
join a religious Order, suggested that perhaps membership in
the Order of Penance of St. Dominic might be the answer.
But Fra Luigi, the Prior of the Dominican convent, remonstrated with them.

"Why did you put that idea into the poor child's head?" he
objected. "You know perfectly well that only widows of a
mature age are eligible to join. It is true that occasionally an
exception is made for an elderly married woman, provided
her husband gives public consent, but young women—married or single—never!"

Father Prior was correct in his statement. He was quoting
the same law which, a half century later, would for a long
time prevent St. Catherine of Siena from becoming a Mantellata. But the friends of Margaret were persistent.

"Surely, Father, when that law was made the lawgivers
were not thinking of one so afflicted as little Margaret. Young
girls are frivolous and they might cause scandal, but
Margaret is not that type, and her physical handicaps
preclude any danger of scandal."

It was this consideration which finally prevailed. But Fra
Luigi insisted on strict observance of the rest of the regulations. Accordingly, a committee of women was appointed to
make a careful investigation into Margaret's faith, character,
and reputation. The report was favorable, and Margaret was
notified, to her unbounded joy, that she was acceptable as a

member, and that she should present herself on the following Sunday afternoon at the Chiesa della Carita for formal admission into the organization. This decision was historic, because, as far as records show, it was the first instance of a young, unmarried woman being permitted to join the Order of Penance of St. Dominic.

The day of her reception was one that always remained sacred in the memory of the blind girl. The church was filled with Dominican friars, members of the Mantellate, and other friends of Margaret. The Prior himself presided at the ceremonies. On the predella of the main altar a throne had been placed; it was here that Fra Luigi took his position. Lying folded on the altar itself was the Dominican habit that was to be given to Margaret.

The blind girl was conducted to the foot of the altar steps, where she knelt. The Prior began the ceremony by asking the formal question:

"What do you seek?"

The girl answered, according to the ritual:

"God's mercy and yours."

The Prior solemnly addressed her in these words:

"Sister Margaret! You are about to become a member of the Order of St. Dominic. Such a step carries with it the gravest obligations. Henceforth, though you live in the world, you must not be part of the world. Your religious habit will be at once a solemn pledge, and a constant reminder, that you have dedicated yourself to the service and love of God, without reserve or conditions other than expressed in the written Rule.

"From now on, Sister, your greatest concern must be to serve God (and your fellowman, out of love of God) to the maximum degree. The attainment of this ideal is possible only if you make your life one of constant prayer, continual mortification and cheerful sacrifice.

"May the spotless white habit you are about to receive be preserved without stain by you until death!"

Turning to the altar, Fra Luigi blessed the religious habit which was on the altar, and handed it to the two Mantellate who were standing beside Margaret. They in turn clothed the girl with the white robe and the black mantle of the Order, while the whole assembly sang the *Veni Creator Spiritus.*

The climax of the ceremony strikingly resembled the manner in which a knight took the oath of fealty to his seigneur.

Fra Luigi took his seat on the throne placed before the altar. The two Sisters led the blind girl up to the altar steps, directly in front of him. Here Margaret knelt, placed her hands on those of the Prior, and in a voice charged with emotion made her profession:

"To the honor of Almighty God, Father, Son and Holy Spirit, and of the Blessed Virgin Mary, and of St. Dominic, and in the presence of you, most reverend Father, Prior of the Order of St. Dominic in Citta di Castello, I, Sister Margaret, do make my profession."

Abruptly her voice broke. She felt that if her happiness were to become any greater she would surely die. After a moment or two she regained control of herself, and now her voice, firm and earnest, rang through the church:

"And I do promise that henceforth I will live according to the form and Rule of the same Order of Penance of St. Dominic, until death!"

As the two Sisters guided Margaret down the altar steps, all the Mantellate surged forward, eager to give her the *Pax,* or Kiss of Peace, for from that day forth the homeless beggar was their very own Sister in Christ.

The Prior stood at the foot of the altar, and raising his arms to Heaven, invoked a blessing on the new Mantellata:

"May He who has begun this good work in you perfect it until the day of Christ Jesus!"

Chapter XIII

THE NEW DOMINICAN TERTIARY

Margaret had always felt that she was alone in the world. Even when she had joined the community at St. Margaret's, the feeling had persisted. Wearing the Dominican habit, she knew that now she possessed what had been lacking in her life. Now, for the first time, she knew what it meant to be part of a family, a great religious family, whose numerous friars and nuns were truly her brothers and sisters by a tie closer than that of blood relationship.

But it was something more than the sense of "belonging" which caused Margaret's heart to sing. It was the ideal of the Order she had joined. No longer was she given the advice that sounded so strange to her:

"Margaret, you must serve God in moderation. The Rule was written centuries ago . . . Times have changed . . . We are more broadminded today. . . ."

Instead, day and night, the emphatic words of the Dominican Prior seemed to echo and re-echo in her ears:

"Your Dominican habit will be a solemn pledge and a constant reminder that you have dedicated yourself, without reserve or conditions, to the love and service of God." Serve God without reserve, without any conditions! This was the language she had been longing to hear. And she was to hear it, repeated over and over in varying ways, at the frequent conferences given to the Mantellate. She listened with the closest attention to these weekly discourses and soon had a complete understanding of the Dominican system of spirituality.

The Rule, she learned, emphasized three things: study, prayer, and penance. A life of study applied, of course, only to the friars of the First Order, but prayer and penance were obligatory for all Dominicans, whether of the First, Second, or Third Order.

The Dominican emphasis on prayer had a special appeal

69

for Margaret, because from childhood she had had the
strongest confidence in the power of intercession before God.
In addition to the prayers prescribed by the Rule, Margaret
daily recited the 150 Psalms of David, the Office of the
Blessed Virgin, and the Office of the Holy Cross. All these
she said from memory. The medieval biographer states—
without giving any details—that she learned these prayers in
a miraculous way.

While Margaret devoted no little time every day to vocal
prayers, it may truthfully be said that they were merely the
interludes in a higher form of prayer, that of meditation. She
never tired, apparently, of reflecting on the various incidents
in the life of Christ, but her favorite subject was the Incarnation and birth of the Savior. She was enraptured by the
thought of an omnipotent God coming to mankind under the
guise of a helpless Infant, and entrusting Himself to the care
of two human beings, Mary and Jseph.

From the time she became a Mantellata, evidence was not
wanting that Margaret began to pass more and more from
mental prayer to the highest form of prayer, that of contemplation. But if the Dominican ideal of prayer found a perfect response in the heart of the blind girl, the Dominican
ideal of penance, clarified for Margaret in one of the first
conferences she heard in the Chiesa della Carita, was no less
welcome.

It was explained to her that St. Dominic had been,
throughout his life, an assiduous reader of the Epistles of St.
Paul, and as a result was strongly influenced by the Apostle's
insistence on the necessity of mortification, if one wished to
conquer the inordinate affections of corrupt human nature
and thus gain "an incorruptible crown."

"That is why," declared the Prior, Fra Luigi, "the saint
adopted for himself and for his Order certain fixed penances:
the daily use of the discipline, interrupting sleep at midnight
to recite Matins and Lauds, the fast from September to the
following Easter, and lastly, the chanting of the Divine
Office in place of the easier private recitation.

"But there was one penance," continued the friar, "which
St. Dominic did not share with his Order; he reserved it for

himself. It was the hardest of all mortifications—lack of sufficient sleep. Every night, after his friars had gone to bed, Dominic would go to the church, and there, before the Blessed Sacrament, spend the long hours of the night in prayer. When exhausted nature at last forced him to take some repose, he would lie on the stone floor of the sanctuary for a few hours' sleep."

So profound an impression was made on Margaret by this conference that it influenced her to the end of her life. After the services had ended and the other Mantellate had gone home, she remained in the silent church pondering on what she had just heard. It had provoked thoughts which, after her usual manner, she wished to consider carefully before making any decision.

She began with the question of Matins and Lauds. The friars arose every night of the year, shortly after midnight, to recite Matins and Lauds. The Mantellate were bound to this penance only on Sundays and on some 70 feast days. Having said the prescribed prayers, they returned to sleep.

But from the moment Margaret had heard the Prior's enumeration of St. Dominic's penances, she felt that she was not doing enough. "It is fitting," she thought, "that the other Mantellate, who are elderly women, most of them with families, should make use of the dispensations granted by the Rule. But it would certainly be slothful for me, a young woman, to pass the night in sleep, while all over the world my brother friars and sisters in the monasteries and convents are singing in choir the praises of God. If I cannot live in a convent, at least I can follow as far as possible the routine of one!"

Accordingly, every night, when Margaret heard the bell of the Dominican monastery announcing the hour for Matins, she would arise to join in spirit with her brothers in their prayers. But the thought of the prolonged vigils of St. Dominic spurred her to do far more. She gave up going back to sleep after her midnight prayers; instead, she would pass the rest of the night in meditation.

Not content with this long and trying vigil, as soon as the bell for Prime was sounded, Margaret would arise from her knees, and taking her cane, tap her way through the dark deserted streets to the Chiesa della Carita, where she would daily go to confession and hear Mass. This remarkable program of mortification the blind girl faithfully carried out until her final illness.

In his conference to the Mantellate, Fra Luigi had spoken of St. Dominic's using the discipline:

"Not only did our holy Father scourge himself, but he did so three times every day: the first time was for any sins which he might have committed against God. The second time was for the salvation of his fellowmen; the third time was to satisfy for the sins of the souls in Purgatory."

As soon as the blind girl obtained permission from her confessor, she began to imitate the saint in this direction. After her death, when the Mantellate were preparing her body for burial, they gazed with awe on the scarred shoulders of the cripple which gave mute testimony that the girl had not spared herself in this penance.

In a word, Margaret not only observed faithfully every detail of the Dominican Rule, but she frequently went beyond the letter of its requirements. She was striving for perfection, and her generous nature refused to count the cost where God was concerned. By reason of her austerities, she was able to keep her body in such absolute subjection that she preserved all her life the vow of virginity she had made at the age of seven. It was not an easy fight for her, because nature had given her a passionate disposition. Yet after her death all her confessors were unanimous in testifying that the girl had led a life of truly angelic purity.

Not all of Margaret's friends looked with approval upon the heroic manner of life she elected to follow. Some of them thought that nature, as well as her parents, had inflicted enough suffering on her without her adding to it. One of these friends was Antonina, who pleaded with her to abandon her program of austerity.

"Antonina," replied Margaret, "what I do is so little compared to what I long to do for God and souls! There are so many souls in danger of perishing for all eternity! Think of the men and women who go through life as if there were no

God and no eternity! Think of all the Christians who live year after year in serious sin! And all these souls were created by God to His own image and likeness—souls so valuable that the Son of God came down from Heaven and died on the cross to save them! And they remain indifferent! Oh, Antonina! If by undergoing suffering I can help save just one of these souls, I would gladly endure the utmost agony from now to the day I die!"

"It is useless to argue with her," thought Antonina in despair. "Her heart is so overflowing with love of others that she has no time to think of herself!"

Despite similar attempts on the part of well-meaning friends, the blind girl continued her austerities and her unending missions of mercy. No sick person was too far away for her to limp to; no hour of the day or night was ever too inconvenient for her to hasten to those in agony. If the sick were in want, she would leave nothing undone to obtain for them the medicine and food they needed.

To the dying, she tried to impart resignation and courage. If they were unrepentant, she would plead piteously with them to make their peace with God; when her pleas brought no response she would turn to prayer. It was rare that even the most hardened sinner succeeded in resisting her efforts, and after every such struggle, Margaret would betake herself, pale and exhausted, to the church to thank God for His mercy.

But the blind cripple did not restrict her apostolate to the sick and dying. If anyone began a conversation with her, Margaret would try to repay their kindness by raising the person's heart and mind to God, thus fulfilling to the letter St. Dominic's admonition to "speak only to God or about God." Invariably she would pass from the subject of God's love to the Incarnation, and thence to Mary and Joseph. The medieval biographer remarks, with a touch of humor, that she would talk about St. Joseph as long as anyone remained to listen! But there was a reason for this.

Devotion to St. Joseph was not then common in the Western Church. Despite popular statements to the contrary, it was not until the close of the 14th century that the cult began to take root and spread. Margaret, therefore, was one of the pioneers of this particular devotion.

Indeed, from childhood to the day of her death she had the warmest admiration for the quiet, self-effacing saint whose heroic faith and deep humility had enabled him to fill so well his unique vocation—that of taking care of a Child who was God and of a woman who was the Mother of that Child. Margaret was not normally a talkative girl, but her friends soon learned that if they were in a hurry, it was imprudent to mention St. Joseph in her presence!

The people of Citta di Castello frequently saw the blind girl limping her way to the sick and dying. At first the sight filled them with astonishment that anyone so afflicted should occupy herself with the miseries of others. But eventually the realization of Margaret's heroic self-denial and her all-absorbing love of her fellowman transformed the popular attitude toward her into a feeling of reverence and veneration. It is not surprising that her biographer speaks of the beauty of her character as being simply "wondrous," nor is it strange that the people of the town shared his opinion of her.

Nor was the feeling restricted to the townsfolk. The story of Margaret's courage circulated throughout the entire countryside, and many a man and woman who had become discouraged by the trials of life listened to it in amazement. As they listened, they felt a new spirit stealing into their hearts; then, ashamed of their cowardice, they once more took up their burdens with renewed faith and hope. Thus, Margaret's fame spread abroad, and wherever it went, it was like a benediction passing over the land.

Chapter XIV

THE TROUBLED HOUSE OF PEACE

Margaret's difficult manner of living came to a close at the time she became a Mantellata. A well-to-do family named Offrenduccio urged her to come and stay with them. Margaret's new home, like some of the more pretentious residences of the city, had a special name inscribed in large letters near the entrance: *Domus Pacis*—"The House of Peace."

The Offrenducci (as well as the Macreti family who lived with them) appear to have belonged to the higher classes of society, as their womenfolk were given the title "Lady," a term usually reserved to women of gentle birth. The one family was composed of Messer Offrenduccio, his wife Beatrice, and an adult son; the second consisted of Messer Macreti, his wife Ysachina (apparently the sister of Beatrice), and an only daughter, Francesca, who was nicknamed "Ceccha."

The medieval biographer informs us that all was not well in "The House of Peace." What was worse, Margaret was again involved in the disturbance.

The storm center was the young girl, Francesca or "Ceccha." She and Margaret had become close friends, and as a result, the blind girl soon discovered that Ceccha knew very little about religion. Margaret zealously undertook to supply what was wanting. Every day she gave Ceccha religious instructions. She also taught her the Office of the Blessed Virgin as well as a number of the Psalms of David. Learning that her pupil had not been to confession since she was a child (she was now 16 years old) and that she had forgotten how to make a confession, Margaret instructed her on how to go to confession and also on how to make a general confession.

While Messer Macreti and his wife were fond of Margaret, they became rather uneasy about the influence the blind girl was exercising over their daughter. Although the parents

75

themselves were indifferent to religion, they had no objection whatever to the religious instruction Ceccha was receiving; in fact, the reputation of being religious rather helped a girl in securing a desirable husband! But Macreti had noticed that— owing to Margaret's influence—Ceccha was being more and more attracted to the religious life, and neither he nor his wife had any intention of allowing her to become a nun. Like nearly all parents, they had set their heart on arranging an advantageous marriage for their daughter. Indeed, they had in mind the prospective bridegroom—a fine young man who came from an excellent and wealthy family.

Messer Macreti had made some delicate overtures to the parents of the youth; the response had been encouraging. Had Macreti been like most fathers, he would have then and there made formal proposals for the marriage, and on his return home, notified Ceccha that she was to marry the young man (whom she hardly knew) on such and such a date! But Macreti was an indulgent father, and being extremely devoted to Ceccha, he did not wish to force her into a marriage that might be repugnant to her.

Notwithstanding, it was high time that Ceccha be settled for life, as she was 16 years of age and all her companions were already married! So the anxious father held a number of conversations with the girl regarding the proposed marriage. He dwelt on the noble family the youth belonged to, on his wealth, his dependable character, the courage he had already shown in battle, and lastly, how good-looking he was! Ceccha had dutifully listened to her father but manifested a discouraging lack of interest.

Her indifference to marriage had become more pronounced since she had become a close friend of Margaret. The parents suspected that this friendship was not advancing their plans. In this they were quite right. For, in her conversations with Ceccha, Margaret had so eloquently depicted the emptiness of the world and the glory of serving God, that the girl longed to become a Mantellata. She knew well that it would be useless to ask her parents for permission to do so. Margaret then decided that she herself would seek the necessary permission; aware, however, of the opposition she would encounter, she prudently awaited a good opportunity.

One day some visitors called to see Messer Macreti and his wife. Margaret was present. After the usual idle talk it was inevitable that the conversation should turn to the new Mantellata and the organization she had joined. Out of politeness to Margaret, each guest felt constrained to contribute some incident showing the goodness of these Sisters. After hearing a number of such instances, Messer Macreti turned to Margaret:

"You should feel proud of your Sister Mantellate, Margaret, for they are really doing splendid work. You see them even in the most inclement weather going on their errands of mercy to the sick and the dying."

"Yes," agreed Lady Ysachina. "One cannot but admire their unselfishness and courage. We are very happy to have one of those wonderful Sisters in our own home!" And turning, she smiled at Margaret.

"Then I beg both of you," swiftly interjected the blind girl, "that you permit your daughter to become one of us."

Both Macreti and his wife were struck speechless by the unexpected request. Ysachina was the first to recover.

"Hush, Margaret!" she chided. "Our daughter will never wear the religious habit!"

There was an embarrassed silence amongst the guests, but Margaret was not disturbed by the emphatic refusal. She calmly continued, as if Ysachina had said nothing:

"Indeed, Ysachina, it will not be long before both you and your daughter will become Mantellate!"

Despite the seriousness with which Margaret said this, the visitors greeted her statement with so spontaneous a roar of laughter that even Macreti and his wife could not help joining in. It was well-known among all of Lady Ysachina's friends that she was a worldly-minded woman who rarely went to church. Margaret was the only one present who remained serious.

When Messer Macreti was able to talk, he remarked:

"Margaret, this is one time when you have allowed your enthusiasm to run away with you! My wife a Mantellata! When that day comes, I'll join the Cistercian monks!"

"I am not joking," Margaret repeated calmly. "Both you, Ysachina, and your daughter will soon put on the Dominican habit, and you will wear that habit as long as you live."

It was only several months later that Macreti suddenly became sick and died a few days later. Lady Ysachina, broken up by his unexpected death, forsook worldly amusements and turned to religion for consolation. Both she and her daughter begged to be admitted to the Order of Penance of St. Dominic. Concerning Lady Ysachina there was no difficulty, but Fra Luigi hesitated to admit the young woman Ceccha, as this was against the Rule. But when he heard of Margaret's prophecy, he felt it was evidently the will of God that another exception should be made. Accordingly, as the blind girl had foretold, Ysachina and her daughter became Mantellate and they remained faithful members until death.

Only one other incident is related of Margaret while she lived in the home of Offrenduccio. Again trouble, this time of a far more serious nature, came to "The House of Peace," but on this occasion the prophecy made by Margaret was accorded a more favorable reception.

The son of Offrenduccio had been arrested and charged with a serious crime. While the biographer does not state the specific charge, he does furnish a clue to its nature. At the beginning of the 14th century there had spread over Central Italy two new political parties, the Neri and the Bianchi. The factions hated each other with such ferocious intolerance that whichever party was in power, the other incessantly plotted its destruction. The government of Citta di Castello was at this time in the hands of the Neri; accordingly, the Bianchi were striving, by fair means or foul, to overthrow it.

The son of Offrenduccio had consorted so much with the leaders of the Bianchi that he was denounced to the authorities as plotting to overthrow the government—hence his arrest. His parents were terrified at his danger, and with good reason. If he were found guilty, the maximum sentence would be a heavy fine. But if, for any reason whatever, the fine were not paid, their son would be flogged through the city streets and then either branded with a red-hot iron or have a hand cut off. In addition, not only he, but also members of his family, might be banished from the State.

Offrenduccio and his wife Beatrice had every reason for alarm, especially since everybody was of the opinion that their son would be found guilty. The frightened mother poured forth her fears to Margaret, who was deeply moved by her friend's distress. It is one of the many curious paradoxes we find in Margaret's life that she who suffered so severely herself, nevertheless was most sensitive to the unhappiness of others. Her gentle nature could never withstand an appeal for help.

Whenever she was confronted with a problem, she instinctively turned to God for counsel and help. On this occasion, after she had prayed a while, she endeavored to console Beatrice by assuring her that no harm would come to her son. Then, conscious of Beatrice's skepticism, she earnestly exclaimed:

"Do not doubt me, Beatrice. There will be no fine imposed, nor will any of you suffer harm because of this affair. This I promise you."

Her prophecy came true. The medieval biographer states that the young man, to the amazement of all his friends, was acquitted. There was no fine and no one was banished.

We are not told how long Margaret continued to live with the Offrenduccio family, nor why she eventually left their home. It is very probable that the sudden death of Messer Macreti may have broken up the household. But whatever the reason, the blind girl ultimately went to live with the Venturino family. It was destined to be her last home in this life.

Chapter XV

MARGARET AND THE PRISONERS

By the time she had moved into the Venturino home, Margaret's life had indeed run the full cycle of fortune. Born in the castle of a rich Captain of the People, she had slept as an outcast in doorways and stables, and then lived in the homes of the poor; now, she was destined to pass the last years of her life a welcome guest in the palace of a wealthy nobleman.

The Venturino residence was literally a palace. The walls of the numerous rooms were adorned with fine tapestries, some of them imported from France; over the doors were hung heavy draperies, and the floors, instead of being strewn with rushes, were covered with carpets and rugs. Every room had its separate fireplace with a flue to carry off the smoke, while all the windows had glass panes in place of the usual oiled linen. A large, secluded garden with a splashing fountain added the last touch of luxury to the Venturino establishment.

The room assigned for Margaret's use was one of the best guest chambers, sunny and spacious. Although its furniture (in keeping with good taste) was somewhat limited, Lady Gregoria thought it well to guide the blind girl several times around the room, teaching her the location of the various appointments: the three-legged table between the door and the hearth, the bench before the fireplace, and the enormous bed, piled high with feather mattresses and surrounded by heavy curtains as a precaution against the night air which was, according to physicians, very dangerous!

The girl's attention was next called to the predella—the platform—used to climb more easily into bed. A large, iron-bound chest, in which clothing could be kept, completed the room's furniture. As Lady Gregoria placed Margaret's hand on the different items, the blind girl's sensitive fingers swiftly explored each one, while she stored away in her retentive

memory an exact picture of the size, shape, and location of
every article.

Margaret's friends were delighted when they heard about
her new home. They were sure that her happiness was complete because her earnest desire to be a member of a religious
Order had been fulfilled, and she now had a permanent home
in which there was every comfort. But as a matter of fact, the
blind girl was far from happy. As a Mantellata, sworn to
follow in the footsteps of Christ, she felt uneasy in the midst
of all this luxury. Then one day she found a solution to her
problem. She accidentally learned that in the garret there was
a small unused room. Seeking out her host, she asked him
if she might have that room in place of the one she then
occupied.

Messer Venturino was stunned.

"You wish to live in the garret!" he exclaimed, hardly able
to believe his ears. "Margaret, that place is not fit for a
human being. It is very small—hardly larger than a big closet!
It has a low ceiling and it is directly under the roof, so that it
is freezing in winter and stifling in summer."

Margaret declared that that was just the kind of place she
needed, "a plain, simple cell, out of everybody's way."
Although Venturino was anxious to do everything he could to
make Margaret happy, he would not approve of her living in
such quarters. But something happened in the course of the
next several weeks which led him to change his mind. It was
his wife, Lady Gregoria, who called his attention to it; but
Venturino, unable to believe her astonishing statement, then
made it a point to be home day after day when his boys
returned from school.

He found his wife had not exaggerated the matter. As soon
as his boys arrived, Margaret would ask them to recite the
lessons assigned them in class. If any of the boys made the
slightest mistake, Margaret would correct him. This would
not be a remarkable feat if the boys were studying only elementary subjects, but their curriculum included logic, geome-
try, astronomy, music and Latin grammar.

Discussing the matter alone with his wife, Venturino asked
her:

"Did Margaret ever have a tutor?"

"No," answered Gregoria. "It would not have done her much good, even if she had, for her blindness would prevent her from reading."

"I cannot understand it," said Venturino in perplexity. "We all know she is very intelligent and has a wonderful memory, but she certainly could not pick up such accurate and extensive knowledge merely by listening to the conversation of others!"

"Perhaps," suggested his wife, "she obtained that knowledge the same way she learned the Psalter. The afternoon she became a Mantellata, Margaret knew by heart only about a dozen psalms. The next morning she began her practice of reciting from memory the 150 psalms, the Office of the Blessed Virgin, and the Office of the Holy Cross!"

"How did she explain it?"

"All she would say was that the knowledge suddenly came to her!"

The conversation left Venturino thoughtful. After supper he told Margaret she could occupy any room in the house she wanted; that night the happy blind girl, with her few possessions under her arm, moved to the garret.

Messer Venturino's conduct toward Margaret during the years she stayed in his home showed that he deservedly enjoyed his high reputation throughout the city as a man of prudence, kindness, and discernment. The biographer next relates another incident which proves that the nobleman's confidence in God as well as his charity for his fellowman was little short of heroic.

One warm day in late spring, Lady Gregoria and her serving maid were in the garden, both of them engaged in the medieval woman's unending task—weaving cloth. While they were there, Margaret returned from visiting the sick. When she entered the house, she paused near the door and listened for a moment. Her keen ears caught the sound of the looms in the garden; making her way there, she seated herself on a stone bench near Gregoria.

"A little while ago," she said, "I met Sister Venturella and she told me that some of the Sisters visit the city prison every day. When I hinted that I would like to accompany them she became evasive. Why does she not want me to go there?"

"Because it is such a dreadful place, Margaret."

"Isn't that all the more reason for my visiting it? Grigia, my heart bled as I listened to her describe the horrible cells, some of them underground without fresh air or light. Many of the prisoners have neither mattress nor straw but must sleep on the cold, damp stones. Few of them have enough clothing, and some of them are actually starving."

"She said that the sick receive no medical care, even if they are dying. And, Oh! Dear God! All the miserable creatures are chained day and night to the walls as if they were savage wild beasts! Because of the inhuman treatment they get, a number of them have ceased to believe in God."

With that, the girl began to cry. Gregoria laid her hand on Margaret's arm and said:

"I feel the same as you do, Margaret, about these poor people. We Mantellate have repeatedly protested to the authorities, but it has done little good."

"But how can the authorities remain so indifferent?" asked Margaret.

"It is not entirely their fault. Only a debased type of man will become a jailer. As his salary is small, he tries to increase it by various extortions, like demanding a fee every time a prisoner wants to be unchained for a short time. But his worst extortion is selling to prisoners who have money, the food donated by charitable persons."

"But what of the prisoners who have no money?"

"They get what is left," answered Gregoria. "If nothing is left, they starve."

"Oh, dear God!" murmured Margaret.

"You asked me why Sister Venturella evaded your request. She did not want to tell you for fear you would think she was doing something heroic. Because of the lack of sanitary provisions, the prison is pervaded by a frightful stench, and worse still, it is a breeding place of disease. Every year fully half the prisoners die of jail fever."

"Ah!" cried Margaret. "I see why you have never taken me there! You are thinking of your husband and children!"

"Yes," agreed Gregoria. "That is the reason I hesitate to ask my husband for permission to go there. It might not be fair to my family to—" She did not go on.

After a few moments of silence Gregoria glanced up from her weaving at Margaret. The silently moving lips of the blind girl told her that, as usual, Margaret had taken the question to a Higher Authority for a solution.

That evening, when the family gathered around the hearth, Margaret asked Venturino if he could not use his influence with the government to improve conditions at the prison. As she continued to pursue the subject at great length (a thing most unusual for her to do—except when speaking of St. Joseph!), Venturino grew thoughtful. The silence of his wife ever since Margaret had broached the subject convinced him that there was something in Margaret's mind which she was not putting into words. Finally he said:

"Little Margaret, would you like to visit the prisoners?"

"Only if it meets with your full approval," was the girl's answer.

For a while there was silence in the room, broken only by the crackling of the burning logs on the hearth. Venturino seemed to be absorbed in the study of the flickering light of the fireplace. When he spoke, it was in a low, solemn voice.

"When I die," he began, "I do not want our good Lord to say to me, 'Venturino, on earth I was hungry and you gave Me not to eat; thirsty, and you gave Me not to drink; sick and in prison, and you visited Me not.'" Then, turning to his wife, he said, "Gregoria, for some time I have suspected that you, too, wish to visit the prison. I am now giving both you and Margaret my permission to do so."

Thus it came about that, despite the revolting conditions of the prison, Margaret, Gregoria, and a few other Mantellate visited the miserable, half-starved prisoners to bring them food, clothing, and bedding. They procured medical assistance for the sick, and they tried to dispose them all, especially the dying, to make their peace with God.

Every day these white-robed heroines could be seen entering the prison, their arms laden with as many bundles as they could carry. But of all their gifts, none approached in value their restoring to the prisoners a consciousness of their dignity as human beings. For the Mantellate taught them that neither the foulest squalor nor the most inhuman brutality can destroy a dignity created by God and still further ennobled by the Son of God.

Chapter XVI

HOUSE AFIRE!

While she was yet a child, Margaret had set out on a long, arduous journey; at the end of it, she hoped to see her God. All through the years she had pressed on toward her objective. She made use of every possible means, ordinary and extraordinary, which would help her to attain this one great aim of her existence. The blows dealt by life hurt her deeply, but she never wavered in her high resolve; instead, knowing that suffering purifies and deepens love, she accepted all the trials and hardships so that her love of God might become purer and deeper.

And now, after many years of patient, humble suffering, signs were not wanting that she was indeed drawing close, very close, to the God she loved so intensely. One cannot come as near to God as Margaret had without some evidences of the presence of the supernatural manifesting themselves. Twice while she was living with the Offrenduccio family Margaret had foretold the future, and both times the prophecies had been fulfilled. Now, in the Venturino home, further proofs of her nearness to God were forthcoming.

The medieval biographer describes the miraculous recovery of a young girl who was at the point of death. She was the daughter of a niece of Lady Gregoria. Margaret had a special interest in the little girl, since she was her godmother. Early one spring the girl fell sick, and despite the best medical care, her condition grew steadily worse. By the last day of spring it became clear that the crisis was at hand. Accordingly, a number of her relatives, who feared she would not last through the night, decided to watch by the bedside. They saw Margaret just outside the door of the sickroom, kneeling in the hallway, where she remained hour after hour in prayer.

Shortly after midnight the bell of a nearby church rang to summon the monks to Matins. At the sound of the bell the child awoke. Recognizing her relatives standing about the bed, she smiled and said:

"Don't worry any more. I have been cured through the prayers of my godmother, Margaret."

With that she fell asleep. When morning came, she arose, her health completely restored.

The next incident was perhaps even more astounding. Owing to the bitter, penetrating cold of the Apennine winters, it was the custom in the wealthier homes to build huge fires on the hearth. A contemporary poet describes:

> *"The mighty fire within the hall,*
> *From logs piled mountain-high."*

It was a particularly dangerous practice because at that period many houses were still built of wood, and even stone buildings usually had roofs of wooden shingles or thatched straw. The narrowness of most thoroughfares and the wooden balconies so popular in medieval Italian cities easily enabled the flames to leap across a street and spread destruction in new areas. Because of the fire hazards, a stringent law compelled every able-bodied man to drop his work at the first alarm and hurry to fight the blaze.

One winter day such a fire broke out in Venturino's home. The servants tried in vain to extinguish it; one of them, realizing the futility of their efforts, rushed to the street and shouted at the top of his voice:

"Fire! Fire! Help! Fire!"

Quickly the alarm was taken up by a dozen voices:

"Fire! Venturino's house! Fire!"

Men came running from all directions, everyone carrying a bucket of water. Two lines were rapidly formed: in the first, men passed from one to the other the buckets of water; in the second line, the empty buckets were returned to the fountain and the cisterns. Meanwhile, the *Anziano* or Senior Warden of that district, who was in charge of operations, dispatched a man to the town hall to ring the great bell, warning all citizens of the danger. As the cry re-echoed in ever widening circles, more and more volunteers arrived to fight the blaze.

The fire had broken out on the ground floor. The volume of smoke, illuminated by darting flashes of fire, and the roar of the blaze as it consumed the old, dried timbers, warned the crowd outside of their peril. People in the adjoining buildings hastily began to remove their most valued possessions to a place of safety. The Anziano, appalled by the violence of the fire, rushed up and down the two lines of men, urging them to greater effort:

"Pass those buckets faster, men! The flames are getting beyond our control!"

Then, seeing Lady Gregoria, who was standing in a doorway, overcome with grief at the loss of her home, the Anziano hurried up to her.

"I am sorry, gracious lady, but I am afraid your house is doomed. It is fortunate that there is no one in the upper rooms."

"Yes," replied Gregoria. "My husband and the children are away for the day . . ." She stopped short, then she gasped, "Margaret! *Madre di Dio!* She did not leave yet for the hospital!"

The next instant she was running as fast as she could into the house, with some desperate idea of going to Margaret's room. She was caught at the foot of the stairs by several men who refused to release her, regarding her plan as suicide.

Unable to tear herself away, Gregoria screamed again and again:

"Margaret! Margaret! The house is on fire! Hurry downstairs! Hurry!"

The blind girl appeared at the head of the stairs. One moment she was concealed by the billows of smoke; the next, she was revealed by the lurid light of leaping flames. The blind girl was not panic-stricken; she was not even excited. Calmly, although she was choking from the smoke, she called downstairs to Gregoria, addressing her by her nickname:

"Grigia, don't be afraid! Have confidence in God! Here, take my cloak and cast it into the flames!"

Margaret removed her black mantle, and rolling it into a bundle, threw it down the stairs. Then she returned to her room in the garret to resume her interrupted prayer. The terrified Gregoria did as she had been told. The medieval biographer tells us what happened next.

"In the sight of the crowd of men who had rushed to Venturino's house to fight the blaze, when the cloak of Margaret was thrown into the flames, the raging fire was instantly extinguished."

. The miracles performed through the prayers of Margaret were obvious indications of the immeasurable spiritual progress she had made. As she drew closer and closer to God, the flame of divine love burned more and more fiercely in her heart. It was because of this intense love that she rejoiced in her infirmities, that she cheerfully and joyously embraced every suffering. She was a striking example of the truth expressed centuries ago by St. Augustine: "When one loves, one does not suffer; or if one does suffer, the very suffering is loved."

Indeed, her joy in suffering was the expression of her boundless love of God and of her neighbor. It was her cheerful, perfect conformity to the divine Will which misled many of her friends into thinking that she did not suffer from her blindness or from her other handicaps. A striking instance of this was the case of Sister Venturella, one of the Mantellate.

Sister Venturella was afflicted with a tumor of the eye which threatened to make her blind. She went to a well-known physician, "the son of Maestro Imberti," who, after examining the tumor, said that he was doubtful whether he could save her sight. He offered to try, however, but the fee he demanded for the proposed treatment was so high that it was entirely beyond the means of Sister Venturella.

Unable to afford the medical treatment, and filled with anguish at the thought of going blind, the unhappy woman hastened to Margaret. Probably the exquisite irony of the situation never occurred to her; she was seeking consolation for her probable loss of sight from a person who had never enjoyed sight! But Margaret refrained from calling Venturella's attention to the fact; instead, she listened with sympathy to her friend.

When the anguished woman had finished her story, Margaret softly said:

"Sister, God is offering you a great gift—a wonderful gift!"

"A wonderful gift? Blindness?" gasped Venturella.

"Yes. He is offering you an opportunity to come much

closer to Him. Oh, my dear friend, accept it! Accept it!"

"Accept blindness? Never! Oh, how can God be so cruel?"

Margaret was silent for a moment; then, in her gentlest tones, she said:

"Sister, did you not take your little boy, Carlo, to the surgeon for a painful operation? How could you have been so cruel?"

"But I did that so he would not be a cripple all his life; I did it out of love for him."

"Nor does God want you to be a spiritual cripple all your life! He, too, is acting out of love for you. Sister, reflect: the suffering will be only for a few short years, but what you gain by the sacrifice will be yours forever!"

"No, no, no! God is asking too much," sobbed the almost hysterical woman. "Never again see the faces of my children? *Dio mio!* I would rather die first!"

Margaret sighed. How many people who had eyesight were blind to the only things that really mattered! Realizing that further argument was hopeless, Margaret stretched out her right hand.

"Sister, will you please place my hand over your eye?"

Thinking that the blind girl wished to learn the size of the tumor, Venturella did as Margaret requested. "The instant Margaret's hand touched the diseased eye," narrates the medieval biographer, "the tumor disappeared and Venturella's sight became perfect."

It was natural that when Margaret made her two predictions about the future (one concerning Lady Ysachina and her daughter, the other concerning the acquittal of Offrenduccio's son), most of the people were of the opinion that she had made lucky guesses. But when her mantle put out the fire in Venturino's house and her hand cured Venturella's eyes, even the skeptics admitted that these things were done by supernatural power. Margaret shrank from publicity, but as she continued to work one miracle after another, it became impossible for her to remain hidden from the public gaze.

The medieval biographer, with the annoying brevity he so often indulges in, does not state what the other miracles were; he merely mentions that, by reason of them, Margaret became celebrated throughout the land, and he adds that "many other things concerning her sanctity should be truthfully told." Evidently he felt that it was unnecessary to put down in writing those extraordinary deeds about which, after a quarter of a century, the people of Citta di Castello were still marvelling.

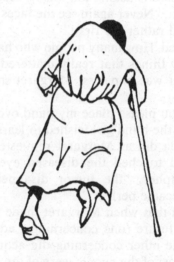

Chapter XVII

MARGARET FINDS A PERMANENT HOME

While the ministrations of the Mantellate had won the hearts of despairing prisoners and induced most of them to accept their sufferings with resignation, there were some men who had suffered such gross miscarriages of justice that they lost, if not their faith in God, at least their belief in His love and mercy.

Alonzo of San Mario was one of them. He had been arrested when his brother, suspected of treason, had fled before he could be seized. In vain Alonzo protested his own innocence and declared he knew nothing of his brother's activities. By the accepted rules of every nation of that period he was put to torture in an effort to force him to reveal his brother's whereabouts. But Alonzo could not tell what he did not know. Finally, permanently crippled by the tortures, he was flung into a dungeon.

When news reached him that, because of his prolonged imprisonment, his wife and little son Antonino were reduced to utter destitution, Alonzo's despair may be imagined; some months later, when he learned that his little boy had died of starvation, the man went almost insane. His blasphemous ravings against the justice and mercy of God made the blood of even hardened criminals run cold. Again and again, in his frenzy of despair, he tried to kill himself. Once when a Mantellata endeavored to comfort him by speaking of God's love for mankind, his language was so frightful that the woman fled in horror.

Margaret and Lady Gregoria had been warned by the other Mantellate that Alonzo would not blaspheme in their presence provided they did not mention God to him. Hence, on their first visit they carefully refrained from saying anything that might arouse the man's rage. But while they knelt beside him to administer to his needs (because of his injuries he was lying prostrate on the floor), the Mantellate were deeply dis-

tressed more by the prisoner's mental and spiritual condition than by his physical sufferings.

On their next visit the two women realized from the curtness of Alonzo's replies that he was with difficulty restraining himself from his usual blasphemies. While Gregoria continued to kneel beside him, bathing his skin ulcers with warm water, Margaret rose to her feet. Bowing her head in prayer, she joined her hands before her breast. Something in her action vividly reminded Alonzo of his dead son, Antonino. Perhaps it was the memory of seeing his little boy assume the same position to say his night prayers. Whatever it was, it caused Alonzo to choke with uncontrollable grief, and he turned his head to the wall lest the other prisoners should witness his agony.

But in another moment a succession of loud gasps and cries of fright caused him to look around the large dungeon. Terror was unmistakable in those cries of "Gesu, have mercy! *Dio mio! Madre di Dio!*" As his glance travelled around the room he saw evident fright on the faces of all the prisoners who were staring in his direction. Puzzled by their fear, he turned his head still further, and then he too gasped in amazement.

A few moments before, Alonzo had seen Margaret standing beside him. But now her body had risen some 20 inches from the ground and remained motionless in the air without any support. Her hands were still joined in the attitude of prayer, but her head was now thrown back as if she were looking through the roof of the prison. It seemed ages to the prisoners before she began to descend slowly to the ground. It was only then that they saw her face. Her face, normally ugly, was now transformed by a glorious radiant beauty that was not of this earth.

Alonzo was staring at Margaret as if he were bereft of his senses; the wall of bitterness, the hatred of God and man which he had built around himself during the last dozen years, was badly cracked by the phenomenon he had just witnessed. Gregoria, encouraged by what she saw in his eyes, whispered to him:

"Dearest brother, you have made our sweet Lord wait for

you a long, long time."

Mechanically, from sheer force of habit, Alonzo tried to blaspheme, but no words came to his lips. He tried to recall his deep grievances against God, but they seemed suddenly to have become elusive. Then, as Margaret once more knelt beside him, he heard himself saying in a choked voice:

"Little Margaret, please pray for me."

The ecstatic prayer followed by elevation from the ground was not an isolated phenomenon with Margaret. From childhood she had always been devoted to prayer, but now she was being swept to the heights of contemplation every day. It was noticed that this profound contemplation was frequently induced whenever she was in the presence of great misery and suffering, for then her thoughts would instantly turn to the sufferings the Savior underwent on earth, and at once she would become—by reason of the intensity of her meditation—utterly oblivious of everything about her. This happened to her nearly every time she visited the prison. It was witnessed not only by the prisoners, but also by many reliable persons who gave sworn testimony concerning it. Indeed, as the story spread through the city, many persons (some of them skeptics) overcame their repugnance to the prison and began to haunt it in order to see the extraordinary phenomenon. The medieval biographer remarks that it was in keeping with divine Goodness that she who sought freedom from all mundane ties should not be held a complete captive to the earth.

Margaret sought to purify her sinless conscience from even the shadows of imperfection by going to confession every day and by receiving Holy Communion as often as she was allowed. During the last years of her life, she revealed to her confessor that whenever she attended Mass she could see Christ Incarnate at the altar. Her confessor sought to give this statement a spiritual meaning.

"Do you mean, Margaret, that you are conscious in some special way of the Divine Presence?"

"No," replied Margaret. "That is not what I mean. I see our Lord."

"But how is that possible, when you are blind?"

"I do not know," was the unperturbed reply.

The confessor was silent for a moment, pondering her statement. Then he said:

"Margaret, do you see the crucifix, the missal, the candles on the altar?"

"No, Father."

"Do you see the priest or the altar itself?"

"No, Father."

"There you are!" he exclaimed triumphantly. "You do not actually see our dear Savior; apparently in some way you sense His Presence. This I can readily understand. There are a number of well-authenticated cases of some"—he was about to say "saints," but he knew Margaret would vehemently protest that she was not a saint—"of some good people having such a gift."

Margaret remained silent.

"Isn't my explanation correct, Margaret?"

"Father," she replied with the utmost tranquility, "you have commanded me to reveal to you in confession the innermost secrets of my heart. Since I am obliged to speak, I must repeat what I have said before: from the Consecration until the Communion I do not see the priest, the crucifix, the missal, or anything else. But I do see Christ our Lord."

Now the confessor was not only a theologian but he had had long experience in directing souls; as a result, he was skilled in distinguishing between genuine mystical phenomena and hallucinations. For many months it had been his duty as Margaret's confessor to subject her to severe, searching tests in order to learn chiefly the state of her soul, because he saw that she had reached exalted heights of spirituality. As it was important to clarify her assertion, he began his approach from another quarter.

"Tell me, Margaret, what does our Lord look like when you see Him during the Mass?"

"Oh, Father," she exclaimed in dismay, "you are asking me to describe Infinite Beauty!"

But despite her protests, her consuming love of God impelled her to begin, with all the fervor of her soul, her canticle of love. As the Dominican theologian critically listened to her glowing attempt to describe Divine Beauty, he had the feeling that the gross material world of the present was fading away and becoming shadowy and unreal, while the veils of eternity were being removed one by one, affording him glimpses of distant supernatural glories. The last shadow of doubt fled from his mind, and with awe he recalled the words:

"Blessed are the clean of heart, for they shall see God."

As the year 1320 began, Margaret's closest friends realized that she was not going to remain much longer in their company. Her twisted little body was obviously losing the fight in its efforts to keep body and soul united. The signs were unmistakable. Margaret was by now so transformed that she had completely forgotten self and thought only of God and His glory.

Theologians teach that when a person's love of God becomes absolutely purified of all selfishness and reaches its maximum intensity, the physical body can no longer hold the soul fettered to it. Margaret's soul had now reached that stage, and every day saw her spirit struggling more and more determinedly to free itself. In her ecstasies, God had evidently revealed something of Himself to her. What she had been permitted to see of the infinite perfections of Eternal Beauty had inflamed the soul of Margaret to such a degree of intense love that it was reacting on her wasted body like a violent fever.

The very violence of the conflict aggravated her illness, but although she suffered greatly, no word of complaint, no expression of pain, ever crossed her lips. But the serene look on her face and the smile always hovering about her lips deceived none of her intimate friends. Margaret herself recognized the approach of death with a joyful tranquility; her long exile from God was coming to a close. She requested Lady Gregoria to send word to the Dominican friars so that, as a daughter of St. Dominic, she might receive the Last Sacraments from a son of St. Dominic.

Quickly the news spread through the town:

"Little Margaret is dying!"

The Mantellate hurried to Venturino's house to pray for their companion in her last hours. Men and women gathered outside the house and anxiously awaited news of their friend. Some were speaking with subdued voices, recalling instances of her unfailing kindness, her invincible patience, her remarkable courage. Others were kneeling in the street praying, as unashamed tears coursed down their cheeks.

Presently they heard from far off a faint murmur that grew ever louder and finally resolved itself into men's voices chanting the Gradual Psalms. In the distance a procession of Dominican friars came into sight. They formed the escort to the Prior, who was bringing the Blessed Sacrament to the dying girl.

The medieval biographer confesses that it is beyond his power to describe the supreme love and devotion with which Margaret received the last rites of the Church. After Margaret had been anointed, the priest held up the Sacred Host before the dying girl. In accordance with the Dominican rite, he solemnly asked her:

"Do you believe that This is the Christ, the Savior of the world?"

Margaret, her face radiant with love, fervently answered: "Yes, I believe it."

The priest then placed the Host upon her tongue, saying:

"May the Body of Our Lord Jesus Christ preserve you until life everlasting!"

The friars and the Mantellate began the prayers for the dying, but Margaret did not hear them. She was rapt in loving contemplation of the God who had come to her in the Holy Eucharist. She could not bear to be separated again from Him Whom she loved so completely; she longed to be dissolved and to be with her Eternal Love forever. Flesh and blood could no longer hold so ardent a soul, and Margaret's spirit, freed at last from its shackles, soared aloft to her God.

The date was the Second Sunday after Easter, April 13, 1320.

Margaret was 33 years of age.

Chapter XVIII

THE MIRACULOUS CURE

Now that Margaret was dead, one might suppose that her remains were consigned to their final restingplace in peace and quiet. But this was not to be. After her stormy life, it was at least consistent that her funeral should not be peaceful, but disturbed by a violent argument.

The Mantellate, in accordance with their Rule, took charge of the funeral. It was their duty to wash the body of the deceased and then clothe it in the religious habit of the Mantellate. There was no embalming, as the only method then in use was so costly that only the rich could afford it. Nor was Margaret's body placed in a coffin; that, too, was expensive. As Dominicans were obliged by their Rule to observe voluntary poverty during life, so in death they were to be buried as the poor were buried; for that reason, no coffin was provided for the burial. Margaret's black Dominican cloak, in which her body was wrapped, would serve as her shroud.

It was customary in those warm climates for the deceased to be buried on the same day on which he died, unless, of course, the death occurred late in the afternoon or in the evening. Hence, without further delay, the customary funeral procession was formed. First walked the Mantellate, each one holding a lighted candle. Next came the pallbearers, carrying the body of Margaret on a wooden frame. A large number of mourners completed the procession.

Ordinarily, the body of a deceased person was taken to the parish church for the funeral rites, but Margaret had expressed her wish to be buried from the Dominican church, a privilege she could claim as a member of the Mantellate. Accordingly, her body was taken to the Chiesa della Carita. When the cortege reached the church, it was found that although Margaret had been dead for only a few hours, the news had spread throughout the city and a multitude of people had hurried to the church to pay their last respects to their friend. So great was the crowd that most of the people had to remain outside in the street, unable to gain entrance to the building.

When the prayers were ended, the friars lifted the wooden frame on which rested the body, and began to carry it toward the side door of the church. Progress was necessarily slow, owing to the dense throng through which the procession had to force its way. As a matter of fact, the friars did not go very far, because as soon as the people perceived what their destination was, cries of protest began to be heard from different parts of the church.

"Don't take her to the cloister! Bury her in the church! She is a saint! Bury her in the church!"

The friars who were pallbearers looked to the Prior for a decision; when he shook his head in the negative, they attempted to continue their course. The people quickly perceived that their wishes were being ignored, and, declares the medieval biographer, they raised "a stupendous uproar." The clamor became deafening.

"She is a saint! She has the right to be buried in the church! Bury her in the church!"

The people were no longer making a suggestion; they were now making a demand. Resolutely they massed themselves between the friars and the entrance to the cloister and they refused to budge. The friars were obliged to halt; it was simply impossible for them to advance one step farther. Again they looked to their Prior for instructions. The latter, by dint of violently waving his arms and by prolonged pleading for silence, finally obtained some semblance of order.

"My good friends," he cried, "like yourselves, we believe that little Margaret was a very holy person. Whether she is actually a saint or not, we have no right to decide; that decision pertains solely to the Church. But have no fear! In due time the Church will make an investigation and then announce its judgment. Meanwhile, I beg of you, my dear friends, to cease this unseemly disturbance. Let us bury little Margaret in the cloister cemetery where the other deceased Mantellate are buried. We can easily transfer the body to a sepulchre in the church after Rome has made an investigation and approved . . ."

The Prior got no further. An enthusiastic admirer of Margaret, Professor Orlando, who taught civil law at the great University of Bologna, sarcastically shouted:

"And how long, Padre, will it take the Church to make the investigation?"

The harassed Prior saw the trap, but he dared not refuse to answer. Perhaps, with luck, he might evade the issue.

"The time varies, Professor. But St. Francis was canonized within two years of his death; St. Anthony of Padua, within one year. That is why I ask you, dear friends, to be patient . . ."

"'Patient' is the right word," vociferated the angry professor. "Thomas Aquinas, Albert the Great, Margaret of Hungary—all of them saints if there ever were any!—have been dead half a century, and Rome is still 'investigating!' We shall be all dead and buried before Rome gets around to Margaret. We citizens of Citta di Castello know full well that little Margaret is a saint. I say, stop this foolishness and bury her in the church."

Orlando was held in high esteem by the citizens because of his great learning, and his impassioned outburst was all that was needed to set off a new and even noisier demonstration. The people, aroused by what Orlando had just told them, renewed their shouting:

"She is a saint! Bury her in the church!"

It was in vain that the Prior and his fellow friars tried to obtain silence a second time. The people were not going to listen. The women were pleading with the friars; the men were arguing and even beginning to shake their fists at the Dominicans. But the friars stood their ground; they were not going to jeopardize Margaret's cause by a hasty, ill-considered action. On the other hand, the people were equally determined not to yield.

The pallbearers grew tired of holding the wooden frame that served as a bier, and they lowered it to the ground until the argument was settled. But no settlement seemed in sight, and the situation, with feeling running higher and higher, might have ended in violence had not the deadlock been broken in a startling way.

A man and his wife had brought to the church their young crippled daughter. She was a mute. But this was only part of her affliction; she also suffered from such extreme curvature of the spine that she had never been able to walk. The parents, carrying their daughter, tried to make their way through the crowd so as to reach the place where Margaret's body was now lying. But progress was impossible until the frantic pleas of the parents to the people in front of them slowly opened a path for them to advance.

Finally the father and mother with their pitiful burden reached the place where Margaret's body rested. They gently placed their afflicted daughter on the ground beside the body, and falling to their knees they began to implore Margaret's intercession for the cure of their child. The tears coursing down the cheeks of the anguished parents moved the bystanders to pity, and they, too, joined in the prayers of the father and mother. The controversy was forgotten. Friars and people alike, with arms raised to Heaven, were pleading for the young girl.

"Margaret! Little Margaret! You yourself were a cripple; have pity on this poor little child! Little Margaret! You are a good friend of God; beg Him to have mercy on this unfortunate!"

The simple warmhearted people spoke what was in their heart: Margaret was their dear friend, wasn't she? While she was alive, had she not loved them deeply? Would she forget her friends now that she was in Heaven? Did she not have the kindest heart imaginable? Was she not always eager to do a kind act? Of course she would listen to them now. She simply could not refuse! And so a veritable hurricane of confident, fervent petitions swelled in volume and swept upward with irresistible force until it reached the Throne of Mercy.

All at once a deep silence fell upon the throng. The people stared as persons do who are afraid their eyes are deceiving them. The left arm of Margaret was rising, reaching over, and touching the young crippled girl beside her. A moment later the girl who had never been able to walk rose unaided to her feet. She stood for a moment as in a dream, as if she could not collect her senses; then a scream re-echoed throughout the church.

"I have been cured! I have been cured through Margaret's prayers!"

Laughing and crying, the girl flung herself into the arms of her father and mother.

The throng in the church went almost delirious with joy.

Chapter XIX

MARGARET'S MISSION

The cure of the mute cripple settled the dispute as to where Margaret was to be buried. The Prior sent for a coffin. When one was finally procured, the body of Margaret was reverently placed in it; then, to the satisfaction and joy of all, the procession returned to the sanctuary of the church.

Meanwhile, the news of the miracle had spread rapidly. The Council of Citta di Castello, assembled at the Palazzo del Podesta, or city hall, decided to make the matter the subject of an official inquiry. The formal investigation found that the girl had been from birth both a mute and a cripple unable to walk; furthermore, that she was now cured of both ailments, and that the cure had taken place in the Chiesa della Carita, at the funeral of Margaret. The report incorporated the sworn testimony of prominent citizens who had witnessed the cure of the mute.

Upon receiving the report, the Council decided that, as a benefactress of the state, Margaret was entitled to special recognition on the part of the government. It was resolved that the body should be embalmed at public expense. Since it was now quite certain that one day the question of Margaret's canonization would arise, the Bishop of the city appointed a number of official witnesses, both lay and clerical, to be present at the embalming.

In view of what will be said later it is well to note here an essential difference between medieval and modern embalming. The modern method uses chemicals which, under favorable conditions, may preserve a body for as long as a dozen years. But in the Middle Ages no preservative chemical was used; the idea was merely to delay decay by removing the viscera and the heart. The spices placed in the body had little or no preservative effect. Under favorable conditions, the medieval method might preserve a body for a week or so, but rarely any longer.

After the embalming, Margaret's body was placed in one of the chapels of the Dominican church, where the people who had loved her in life might visit her in death. It was an opportunity which the people availed themselves of with alacrity, for they were convinced that if Margaret's intercession with God had been so effective while she was on earth, now that she was in Heaven her services would be even more efficacious. Throngs visited her tomb every day, coming not merely from the city, but also from the neighboring republics. That popular confidence in Margaret was not misplaced is evidenced by numerous medieval documents, sworn to before the notary public.

The affidavits are many—over two hundred of them—testifying to permanent cures of the blind, the deaf, the lame, and of those with various other afflictions. As a result, Margaret's fame as a wonder-worker spread throughout central Italy; then it was suddenly overshadowed by an unparalleled international calamity—the outbreak of the plague called the Black Death. The plague devastated all Italy and the rest of Europe for three years, and killed several million people.

But even this appalling slaughter did not quench man's thirst for more killings. Rival European nations made conflicting claims for various areas of Italy and the wars for these territories were fought on Italian soil. For the next several centuries, death and desolation became a way of life for the people of that war-torn land.

It was not until 1600 that Rome finally took official cognizance of Margaret. Clement VIII appointed a committee to investigate her "cause." He placed in charge of the inquiry one of the most erudite scholars in Europe—the Jesuit Cardinal, Robert Bellarmine. After a thorough investigation, the Cardinal submitted his report to the Pope. But Clement was ill, and died before he could read it. His successor, Paul V, studied the report, and on October 19, 1609, beatified Margaret, assigning April 13th as her feast day.

This, then, is the story of Margaret of Castello. It is a story that staggers belief—that parents could be so inhuman as to put into a prison their six-year-old child, keep her there for

14 years, and then abandon the blind girl in a distant city. It would be unbelievable did not reliable historical documents of that same period tell of even greater atrocities perpetrated by some other lords.

By every human standard, Margaret should have become a bitterly unhappy girl, hating everybody and desiring death as the only release from her many miseries. The chaplain at Metola castle realized the tragic life ahead of the girl, but when he discovered what a high degree of intelligence she possessed, he began to have hope for her. He glimpsed the possibility of her rising superior to her handicaps and attaining genuine happiness—if only she had a strong enough faith.

But the odds against her were enormous. She would have to accept and patiently bear her severe handicaps—hunchback, midget, blind, lame and ugly. She was well aware of all of them—thanks to the barbarity of her parents. In addition, she would have to overcome the trauma inflicted on her by the knowledge that her parents did not love her, and even hoped she would die. For her to overcome all these handicaps and gain real and lasting happiness would be nothing short of a miracle. Margaret's claim to undying glory is that she did perform that miracle.

And this was the girl of whom the people of Metola had said it would be better for her to die than to live! It was well that she did live, for during her lifetime her unshaken belief in the love that God has for every individual human being brought fresh hope and courage to hundreds of weary hearts. And after her death, the story of her matchless faith in God's love has been retold again and again down through the centuries, and it has inspired with new courage thousands who, discouraged by adversities, felt that life was not worth living.

This is why an obscure girl, who occupied no prominent place in political life, who possessed no outstanding talents with which to gain the attention of the world, has nevertheless lived in the memory of man for over six hundred years.

It is also the reason why she will undoubtedly continue to remain enshrined in many hearts as long as there remain on earth such things as Faith, Hope—and Love.

NOVENA PRAYERS
in honor of
BLESSED MARGARET OF CASTELLO
Dominican
1287 - 1320

"For my father and my mother have left me: but the Lord hath taken me up."

—Psalm 26:10

Nine consecutive days of prayer asking Blessed Margaret of Castello's intercession with God for our needs.

FIRST DAY

O Blessed Margaret of Castello, in embracing your life just as it was, you gave us an example of resignation to the Will of God. In so accepting God's Will, you knew that you would glorify God, grow in virtue, save your own soul, and help the souls of your neighbors. Obtain for me the grace to recognize the Will of God in all that may happen to me in my life, and so to resign myself to it. Obtain for me also the special favor which I now ask through your intercession with God.

Let us pray

O God, by whose Will the blessed virgin, Margaret, was blind from birth, that the eyes of her mind being inwardly enlightened, she might think without ceasing on Thee alone, be the light of our eyes, that we may be able to flee the shadows of this world and reach the home of never-ending light. We ask this through Christ Our Lord. Amen.

Jesus, Mary, Joseph, glorify Thy servant Blessed Margaret by granting the favor we so ardently desire. This we ask in humble submission to God's Will, for His honor and glory and the salvation of souls.

(Say one Our Father, Hail Mary *and* Glory Be to the Father *after each day's prayer.)*

SECOND DAY

O Blessed Margaret of Castello, in reflecting so deeply upon the sufferings and death of our Crucified Lord, you learned courage and gained the grace to bear your own afflictions. Obtain for me the grace and courage that I so urgently need so as to be able to bear my infirmities and endure my afflictions in union with our Suffering Savior. Obtain for me also the special favor which I now ask through your intercession with God.

Let us pray: O God, etc.

THIRD DAY

O Blessed Margaret of Castello, your love for Jesus in the Blessed Sacrament was intense and enduring. It was there, in intimacy with the Divine Presence, that you found the spiritual strength to accept sufferings with cheerful serenity, patience, and kindness toward others. Obtain for me the grace to draw from this same Source, as from an inexhaustible font, the strength whereby I may be kind and understanding of everyone, despite whatever pain or discomfort may come my way. Obtain for me also the special favor which I now ask through your intercession with God.

Let us pray: O God, etc.

FOURTH DAY

O Blessed Margaret of Castello, you unceasingly turned to God in prayer with confidence and trust in His fatherly love. It was only through continual prayer that you were able to accept your misfortunes, to be serene, patient, and at peace. Obtain for me the grace to persevere in my prayer, confident that God will give me the help to carry whatever cross comes into my life. Obtain for me also the special favor which I now ask through your intercession with God.

Let us pray: O God, etc.

FIFTH DAY

O Blessed Margaret of Castello, in imitation of the Child Jesus, who was subject to Mary and Joseph, you obeyed your father and mother, overlooking their unnatural harshness. Obtain for me that same attitude of obedience toward all those who have legitimate authority over me, most especially toward the Holy Roman Catholic Church. Obtain for me also the special favor which I now ask through your intercession with God.

Let us pray: O God, etc.

SIXTH DAY

O Blessed Margaret of Castello, your miseries taught you better than any teacher the weakness and frailty of human nature. Obtain for me the grace to recognize my human limitations and to acknowledge my utter dependence upon God. Acquire for me that abandonment which leaves me completely at the mercy of God, to do with me whatsoever He wills. Obtain for me also the special favor which I now ask through your intercession with God.

Let us pray: O God, etc.

SEVENTH DAY

O Blessed Margaret of Castello, you could so easily have become discouraged and bitter, but instead you fixed your eyes upon the Suffering Christ, and there you learned from Him the redemptive value of suffering—how to offer your sufferings to God in reparation for sin and for the salvation of souls. Obtain for me the grace to endure and value the power of my sufferings in union with Christ on His Cross for the needs of others and the world. Obtain for me also the special favor which I now ask through your intercession with God.

Let us pray: O God, etc.

EIGHTH DAY

O Blessed Margaret of Castello, how it must have hurt when your parents rejected and abandoned you! Yet you learned from this that all earthly love and affection, even for those who are closest, must be sanctified. And so, despite everything, you continued to love your parents—but now you loved them in God. Obtain for me the grace that I may see all my human loves and affections in relation to and for God. Obtain for me also the special favor which I now ask through your intercession with God.

Let us pray: O God, etc.

NINTH DAY

O Blessed Margaret of Castello, through your suffering and misfortune, you became aware of and sensitive to the sufferings of others. Your heart reached out to all those in trouble—the sick, the hungry, the dying, and prisoners. Obtain for me the grace to recognize Jesus in everyone with whom I come into contact, especially in the poor, the rejected, the unwanted! Obtain for me also the special favor which I now ask through your intercession with God.

Let us pray: O God, etc.

FINAL PRAYER

O my God, I thank Thee for having given Blessed Margaret of Castello to the world as an example of the degree of holiness that can be attained by anyone who truly loves Thee, regardless of his natural deficiencies, by cooperating with Thy grace.

In our times, Margaret, like so many others, would almost certainly have been destroyed by abortion or infanticide, her parents being more concerned with the circumstances of their lives than with the needs of her poor, frail, and twisted body.

But Thy ways are not the world's ways. And so it was Thy Will not only that Margaret should be born, but also that through the faith and goodness which her beautiful and loving heart magnified, Thy power and wisdom should be manifested to this egocentric and unbelieving world.

By Thy wisdom, Margaret's blindness allowed her to see, search, and love Thee more clearly. A cripple, she leaned and depended upon Thee more completely. Dwarfed in physical stature, by Thy grace she became a giant in the spiritual life; deformed in face and body, she was united with the rejected and outcasts, and with Jesus on the Cross.

Her life dramatized the words of the Apostle Paul: "Gladly therefore will I glory in my infirmities, that the power of Christ may dwell in me. For which cause I please myself in my infirmities, in reproaches, in necessities, in persecutions, in distresses, for Christ. For when I am weak, then am I powerful." (2 *Cor.* 12:9-10).

I beseech Thee, O God, Father, Son and Holy Spirit, to grant that, through the intercession of Blessed Margaret of Castello, all those handicapped in body and mind, all those whose sins have made spiritually halt, blind, and lame, all those rejected, all the *unwanted* of this world, may, by depending more fully upon Thy power and mercy through prayer, come to boast of their weaknesses in this life, and the sight of Thy glory in the next. Amen.

Blessed Margaret of Castello, pray for us!

(3 *Our Fathers* and 3 *Hail Marys*)

Imprimi Potest: V. Rev. E. R. Daley, O.P.
                      Prior Provincial
Imprimatur: ✟Thomas J. McDonough, D.D.
                      Archbishop of Louisville
                      December 5, 1980

Please report all favors received through the intercession of Blessed Margaret of Castello to:

Coordinator of Blessed Margaret Cause
Priory of St. Dominic-St. Thomas
7200 West Division Street
River Forest, Illinois 60305

or

V. Rev. Fr. Postulator General, O.P.
Convento Santa Sabina
Piazza Pietro d'Illiria, 1 (Aventino)
00153, Rome
Italy

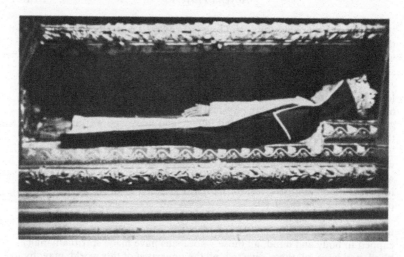

The incorrupt body of Blessed Margaret in a glass sarcophagus at the School for the Blind, Citta di Castello, Italy. Blessed Margaret is dressed in the black and white habit of the Mantellate ("veiled ones"), a group of lay women affiliated with the Dominican Order. She wears a symbolic "crown of heavenly glory." *(Photo courtesy of Roger Sorrentino, Yonkers, N.Y.)*

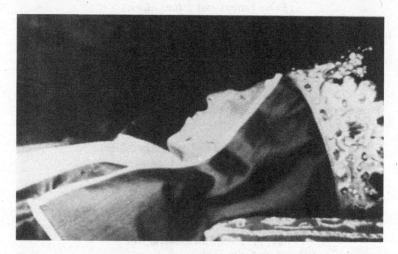

Profile of Blessed Margaret's face, with the flesh intact but discolored after more than 660 years. Effective embalming was unknown in Margaret's time. Traditionally, bodily incorruption is considered by the Church as an indication of divine intervention, and is examined together with other evidence in evaluating the individual's possible "heroic virtue," i.e., sanctity of life. *(Photo courtesy of Roger Sorrentino, Yonkers, N.Y.)*

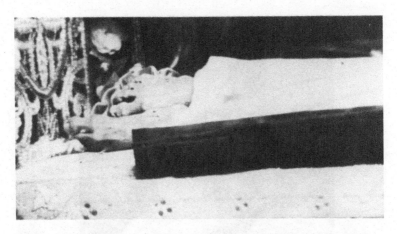

Detail of Blessed Margaret's feet showing some deformity of the left foot, and, despite the camera angle, the relative shortness of her right leg. Margaret's contemporaries described her as facially disfigured, blind, a hunchback and lame. *(Photo courtesy of Roger Sorrentino, Yonkers, N.Y.)*

Archbishop Thomas J. McDonough blesses the new shrine in honor of Blessed Margaret on April 13, 1981, Margaret's feast day and the anniversary of her death. The statue, located at Blessed Margaret's shrine in the Church of St. Louis Bertrand in Louisville, is the work of Tony Moroder of Moroder International, Milwaukee.

ABOUT THE AUTHOR

Father William Raymond Bonniwell, O.P. has had a long, fruitful life, a great part of it spent as a Dominican priest and scholar (ordained in 1914). He has been a renowned preacher and retreat master, and was Director of the Preachers' Institute in Washington, D.C.

Now in his 90's, Father Bonniwell is suffering the infirmities of age, and is nearly blind. He resides at St. Vincent Ferrer Priory in New York City.

Father Bonniwell spent a good deal of time in Italy gathering information on Blessed Margaret. He is very grateful to many persons in Citta di Castello for their unstinting efforts to assist him in his research every time he visited their city. In the region once called Massa Trabaria (Mercatello, Metola, Sant'Angelo in Vado, etc.), the eager cooperation he received resulted in his unearthing valuable data not given by the medieval biographers of Blessed Margaret. To all his Italian "assistants" who helped make this book possible, Father Bonniwell offers his warmest and deepest thanks.

Other works by Father Bonniwell include *Liturgical Spirit of Lent, History of the Dominican Liturgy, Interpreting Sunday Mass, Martyrology of the Sacred Order of Preachers,* and *What Think You of Christ?*